D0467457

WINE to WATER

AVERY

a member of

Penguin Group (USA) Inc.

New York

WINE to WATER

A Bartender's Quest to Bring

Clean Water to the World

DOC HENDLEY

Published by the Penguin Group
Penguin Group (USA) Inc., 375 Hudson Street, New York,
New York 10014, USA • Penguin Group (Canada), 90 Eglinton Avenue East,
Suite 700, Toronto, Ontario M4P 2Y3, Canada (a division of Pearson Penguin
Canada Inc.) • Penguin Books Ltd, 80 Strand, London WC2R 0RL, England •
Penguin Ireland, 25 St Stephen's Green, Dublin 2, Ireland (a division of Penguin Books Ltd) •
Penguin Group (Australia), 250 Camberwell Road, Camberwell, Victoria 3124, Australia (a division
of Pearson Australia Group Pty Ltd) • Penguin Books India Pvt Ltd, 11 Community Centre,
Panchsheel Park, New Delhi–110 017, India • Penguin Group (NZ), 67 Apollo Drive,
Rosedale, North Shore 0632, New Zealand (a division of Pearson New Zealand Ltd) •
Penguin Books (South Africa) (Pty) Ltd, 24 Sturdee Avenue,
Rosebank, Johannesburg 2196, South Africa

Penguin Books Ltd, Registered Offices: 80 Strand, London WC2R 0RL, England

Most Avery books are available at special quantity discounts for bulk purchase for sales
promotions, premiums, fund-raising, and educational needs. Special books or book excerpts
also can be created to fit specific needs. For details, write Penguin Group (USA) Inc.
Special Markets, 375 Hudson Street, New York, NY 10014.

ISBN 978-1-583-33462-1

Printed in the United States of America
1   3   5   7   9   10   8   6   4   2

Book design by Meighan Cavanaugh

Some names and identifying characteristics have been changed
to protect the privacy of the individuals involved.

While the author has made every effort to provide accurate telephone numbers and
Internet addresses at the time of publication, neither the publisher nor the author
assumes any responsibility for errors, or for changes that occur after publication.
Further, the publisher does not have any control over and does not assume
any responsibility for author or third-party websites or their content.

*Penguin is committed to publishing works of quality and integrity.
In that spirit, we are proud to offer this book to our readers;
however, the story, the experiences, and the words
are the author's alone.*

This book is dedicated to my wife, Amber.

Darlin', you are the most beautiful thing in my sometimes dark and crazy world. Thank you for being patient with me during the growing pains of Wine to Water and for loving me despite my many imperfections. I would be nowhere without you.

"Whiskey is for drinking; water is for fighting over."

—*source unknown*

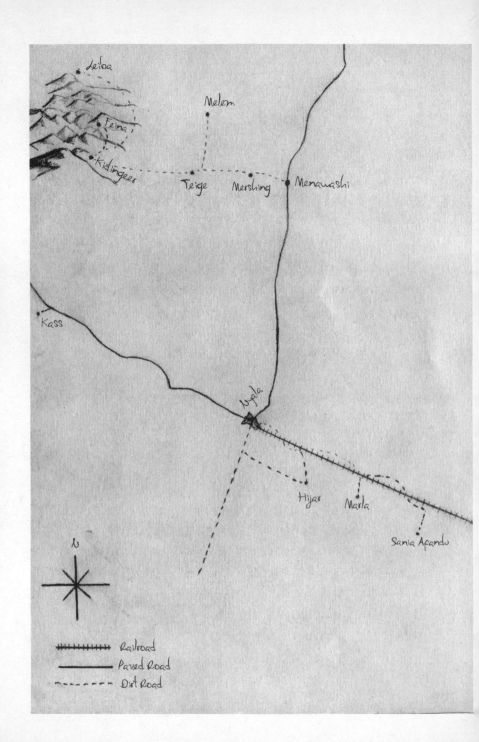

Glossary of Terms

AU—African Union, a union consisting of fifty-three African nations whose mandate is to promote peace, security, and the well-being of the African continent and its peoples

Buffalo—the nickname we gave to our hard-top Land Cruiser

Chai—hot tea

Fool—a traditional Darfuri dish made of whole fried beans served in oil

GoS—government of Sudan

IDP—internally displaced person

Janjaweed—Arab militia believed to be supported by the government of Sudan that has been responsible for widespread killing of the black African population of Darfur

Jebena—coffee

Jellabiya—a traditional Muslim garment worn by men in Egypt and Sudan

JEM—Justice and Equality Movement, rebel group fighting against the Janjaweed and the government of Sudan

NFI—non-food item, i.e., soap, jerricans, plastic sheeting, etc.

NGO—non-governmental organization

OCHA—Office for the Coordination of Humanitarian Affairs, part of the United Nations

Salah—Islamic prayer required five times daily

Seeco—a local Darfuri liquor distilled from date fruit, very similar to moonshine

SLA—Sudanese Liberation Army, rebel group fighting against the Janjaweed and the government of Sudan

USAID—United States Agency for International Development

Wadi—a riverbed in Darfur that is dry most of the year except during the rainy season, when it can flood to dangerous levels within minutes

Names of Characters

Abdulla—the driver of my water truck for Marla Camp

Ali—an SLA commander and community leader based in Marla

Amber Hendley—my beautiful wife and the mother of my two sons, Beattie and Justice

Amir—one of my first hires; a humble Muslim man from Nyala, South Darfur, who spoke very little English but was well trained in water and sanitation

Andy Shaver—a Samaritan's Purse colleague and friend, who worked on education and eventually took over managing all of our Darfur programs

Annie Clawson—a young woman who helped me launch Wine to Water as an official organization back in 2007, and who, thanks to her endless supply of sticky-notes, is the only person who has been able to keep me on task and on a schedule

Coy Isaacs—a Samaritan's Purse colleague in Darfur, sparring partner, and also great friend, who helped me set up the first Wine to Water office in Boone, North Carolina, in 2007

David Del Conte—head of the United Nations' OCHA office in Darfur

Hamid—a young, educated Muslim man from Nyala, South Darfur

Hilary—a proud older Christian man from Wau in South Sudan, who was my main translator and first hired along with Amir

Ismael—a Muslim man from a small village south of Nyala, with decent English skills and well trained in water and sanitation work

Jonathan Drake—a Samaritan's Purse colleague, fellow travel guitar player, and friend who worked mostly on food security

Mohamed Isa—an SLA commander based in Jebel Marra

Simon—a university-educated Christian man from Juba, South Sudan, who helped me with writing grant applications for materials from UNICEF and also helped as a translator

Tasha Sullivan—a close friend from Raleigh, North Carolina, who helped me start Wine to Water and host the first few events back in 2004

Waheed—a teacher from Jebel Marra, who worked on building schools with Andy but also sometimes accompanied me to Jebel Marra as a translator because of his connections

WINE to WATER

ONE

I'd driven this same road through the low desert plains of South Darfur dozens of times before. But this time something was different. Something just didn't seem right.

For the most part, everything looked the same as it always did: endless rust-colored sand, the heavy African sun, scattered sage, brown scrub brush and dark green mukheit bushes, and a smattering of tiny mud huts with thatched roofs on either side of the rough, sandy, two-lane path that actually passes for a proper road here in Sudan, the largest country in Africa.

The thing that really caught my eye as we rolled toward the tiny village of Teige was this: It was the first time I'd actually ever seen humans here. In the past, this small village was nothing more than a skeleton, like some Wild West ghost town. A couple years back, in 2003, there had been heavy fighting here. The Janjaweed eventually took over the place, so the villagers of Teige abandoned their homes and headed for one of the many refugee camps popping up in the desert.

Off in the distance I noticed a handful of men riding on horseback across a low hill, their figures silhouetted by the bright sun. Others were walking slowly along paths between the huts, machine guns slung over their shoulders.

"What the hell?" I mumbled to myself aloud. "These must be the dudes the SLA commander warned me about this morning."

I looked over to my right at Waheed, a teacher in his mid-forties from the nearby mountains of Jebel Marra who was working with me on our water projects. He didn't seem worried at all. Waheed simply stared calmly out the windshield, chain-smoking his Bringi cigarettes.

I was driving a large white four-wheel-drive Land Cruiser we'd affectionately named the Buffalo, mostly for the way it charged along those rough desert roads. Following closely behind was another smaller white Land Cruiser pickup truck with a pair of my men, Ismael and Mohamed. We were on our way back from surveying the water needs of villages in the Jebel Marra region, and headed to our home base in Nyala, in the northern half of South Darfur.

Whenever we had a convoy like this—no matter how large or small—I always drove the lead vehicle. Even though having the white guy leading the charge runs totally counter to every established convoy strategy in the book, I just never felt quite right putting my life in the hands of some local Sudanese guy who'd taught himself to drive only a few years earlier. I also always chose to drive the Buffalo because it was a cushier ride and swallowed the bumpy roads much better than our pickup.

As we rumbled deeper into the village, something caught my eye on the side of the road. About a hundred yards up on the left, I saw a man crouched down. He was dressed in the traditional garb of Arabian nomads, a once white but now dirty yellowish-brown flowing jellabiya, with half his face covered in an equally dirty white head wrap.

After spending nine months working in Darfur, I'd grown accustomed to the occasional roadblock, where SLA rebels or Janjaweed fighters would put their hands out and guns in the air, firing a warning shot. Then I'd drop the name of a local commander or tribal leader to convince them to let us pass. But this time there was no one blocking the road.

We were traveling about thirty mph, so we came upon him quickly. Fifty feet. Forty feet. Twenty feet. As we closed in on the man I clearly saw the barrel of his AK-47 tracking our progress. It felt as though his gun was aimed directly at my face. I also noticed a half dozen other men, some wearing the green camouflage fatigues of the Sudanese army, crouching along either side of the road nearby. All of their weapons were trained directly on us.

Do I keep going? Do I slow down? I asked myself.

My gut answered first and I floored the Buffalo. She lurched and groaned in response, kicking a thick cloud of dust into the air. As soon as our truck was passing the first man, almost exactly perpendicular with him, I watched as he squeezed the trigger. Through the open window I felt the blast send shock waves across my sunburned face. The bullet made a *Pfsick* sound as it flew past and out the passenger-side window.

The gunner was obviously aiming directly at my head, but he must've led us a bit too much. Immediately the other men began shooting too. I caught a glimpse of several men on horseback, charging down the hill toward us in clouds of dust, guns high in the air.

Instinctually I made my body as small as possible, with only my eyes peeking through the gap between the steering wheel and the dashboard. I'd played out situations like this in my mind a hundred times before, but this was the first time the bullets were real.

Pata-pop-pop-pop!

Pfsick-pfsick-pfsick.

Pata-pop-pop-pop!

Pfsick-pfsick-pfsick.

The bullets continued ringing out in spurts of three. I could hear them skimming past my head. The rear window shattered.

I started laughing. Out loud. No matter whether it's a scrap or an emergency or some situation where I should be composed or mad or serious or whatever—when I'm uncomfortable I almost always start laughing.

I was struggling to keep the Buffalo on the road. The desert scrub slammed the truck's undercarriage as I veered too far to the left; then I felt the grinding of deep sand dunes as I careened to the right. I was certain the swaying would soon become too much and flip the truck. But there was no time to worry about that as bullets continued whizzing through the air, a couple more impacting our truck with a *clank-clank-thud.* *Clank-clank-thud,* like hammers slamming into a steel wall.

Oddly, all I could think about was how much this sounded exactly like that scene from the film *Saving Private Ryan* where the American soldiers are ambushed as they storm Normandy.

Man, Spielberg actually got it right. I chuckled to myself.

I continued laughing nervously and uncontrollably as my copilot just stared forward, smoking his cigarette, bullets zipping past our heads. *Pfsick-pfsick-pfsick.*

Dude, I'm gonna flip this thing over. Then they're gonna just come and shoot us in the head, I thought to myself as I tried to will the Buffalo back onto the road again.

Suddenly my shortwave radio crackled alive with the sound of panic from the other truck.

"Boss, boss, we must stop!" yelled Ismael. "They are shooting us like crazy! Our tire is flat! What do we do? Do we pull over?"

"No! Do not stop!" I commanded. "Go five kilometers more and then stop. Just five more clicks. I'll meet you there!"

Eventually the bullets quit. But I didn't dare slow down. I

looked back but couldn't see my men's truck in the side-view mirror, which miraculously hadn't been shot out.

The whole scene happened quickly, maybe three minutes in all, but the truck's odometer turned painfully slowly. By the time all five kilometers had finally clicked past, we crested the top of one last hill and I brought the Buffalo to a stop in a wide, arid valley where I could see clearly all around me.

Waheed just sat there, quietly smoking another Bringi. He seemed way too calm for what we'd gone through. Me— I was amped up like I'd just pounded ten cans of Red Bull. I quit laughing and my mind started racing.

There was no sign of my men and their truck.

Where are they? They're not coming. They're dead, I rattled to myself. *Way to go, dude. You just left your own guys back there to die. Nice frickin' job.*

I grabbed both satellite phones (one on the U.S. Iridium network, the other a Middle Eastern Thuraya phone) and dialed wildly in an attempt to raise someone back at base. I called four times. No answer. So I dialed the number of David Del Conte, a friend and head of the Darfur region of the United Nations' Office for the Coordination of Human Affairs (OCHA), the logistics arm that oversees the entire relief effort here.

No answer. So I redialed. This time he picked up immediately.

"Hello?"

"David, it's Doc!"

"Doc, this had better be good. I'm in Khartoum, in the middle of an important UN meeting."

"Dude, we just got ambushed! I don't know what the hell is going on. There may be loss of life. There may not be loss of life. I don't know what protocol is. One truck in my convoy is missing. I don't know where to go."

"Slow down. Slow down. Just tell me what you need. Where are you, Doc?"

"Um, I think, um, I'm heading east on the road from Jebel Marra."

"Okay. Here's what you need to do: About ten kilometers down the road, in Mershing, is a police station. Know the one?"

"Yeah, I think so."

"I want you to drive straight there and wait."

"But what about Ismael and Mohamed, in the other truck?"

"Give them five more minutes; if they don't arrive by then, head on."

"But the police, they're probably in cahoots with the frickin' Janjaweed. They might just kill us anyway."

"I'll have an AU [African Union] helicopter waiting for you guys at the police station when you get there. Everything is going to be fine."

About the time I hung up with Del Conte, I heard a faint rumble and slap coming up the hill. As it got louder I realized it was my boys. Their front tire had indeed been shot out, the rubber spanking the Land Cruiser's wheel well wildly as it hobbled up the knoll.

We greeted our friends with tire irons in hand. Ismael and Mohamed were clearly shaken up. But still, together the four of us changed that tire like a well-oiled pit crew at a NASCAR race back home in North Carolina.

"Boss, that was not good," said Mohamed. "Not good. Janjaweed for sure."

"Yep, had to be those same guys the SLA commander warned us about," I agreed.

As the men finished up with the tire, I took a quick look at the damage to the Buffalo. When I opened the rear door a large chunk of glass fell on the scorched ground at my feet. There were several bullet holes torn throughout. But what really grabbed me was a tiny strip of cardboard that had been rolled back like a curlicue by a bullet skimming across the top of one of the five large boxes of chlorine tablets we were hauling. The bullet was headed straight through the truck and toward my head, but at the last second its trajectory veered sharply to the right before slamming into the sidewall of the truck. Maybe my crazy-ass driving threw it off. Maybe something else. But whatever it was, this box of ten thousand chlorine tabs destined to clean drinking water that'd save thousands of Sudanese lives had actually, in a way, saved my own life.

All I could think about was, *What the hell is a guy like me doing in the Sudanese desert, getting shot at in the middle of the largest humanitarian crisis of our lifetime?* That's a great question. And one I've asked myself a hundred times over the past year.

I'm a bartender, after all. I'm not an engineer. I didn't get a master's degree in public policy or international development. And before landing in the Sudan in August 2004, I didn't know the first thing about how to drill a well or install a water filter. And I sure as hell didn't know how to solve the water problem in Darfur. All I knew was that there were thousands of people dying on a weekly basis because of the lack of clean water, and I soon found out that approximately 60 percent of the wells that had been installed in the region were inoperable. And there were plenty of refugees, or internally displaced persons (IDPs, as the politicians call them), living in camps with little to no access to clean water.

Though I had no formal training, once in the field I quickly figured out a few things I could easily do to help. First, I learned how to set up a big ol' water bladder and fill it up. Then a UNICEF guy helped me source the tools and pipes needed to start making easy fixes on broken wells in the small villages of the region. The work was hard, but the results were immediate. And immediately gratifying.

That first bladder I installed was in Marla Camp. Unlike the well-funded, well-equipped IDP camps found elsewhere in Darfur, the ragtag tent city of Marla, thirty miles southeast of Nyala, was controlled by the Sudanese Liberation Army (SLA), and smack-dab in the middle of a UN "no-go zone," which means it was deemed too dangerous to allow aid workers in to help. Without outside aid these people were in desperate need of water. That's why I chose to start my work there.

The water bladder, which I also got from UNICEF, looked

like a big white rubber pillow lying lifeless on the ground. It was fifteen feet long by ten feet wide and about two to three feet deep, and capable of holding up to twenty-five hundred gallons of water. I'd also erected a pair of simple tap stands made of galvanized steel. It'd been only twenty-four hours since I laid it out, but already the thing was covered in rust-colored sand. It looked old and dirty. Maybe even a little useless. I wondered myself if it'd even work.

But people from the camp lined up anyway. Hundreds of them. It wasn't even eight a.m. yet and the women and children of Marla Camp, with their dingy yellow jerricans, had already started a pair of queues, one behind each tap stand, lining up for what they hoped would soon be coming. There were no men in that long snaking line, and virtually no men at all living in this camp. I'm not sure why exactly, but likely they were off fighting with the SLA or had already been slain by the fierce Janjaweed fighters.

By midmorning the temperature had already climbed to well over a hundred degrees Fahrenheit, so I hunkered down in the little slice of shade offered by my Land Cruiser. I'd been waiting for three hours and was dozing off when I was snapped awake by the far-off chugging of a diesel truck negotiating the thick sand on its way up the long hill to Marla.

Soon the rusty two-ton truck with a big ol' square hand-welded water tank crested the hill, announcing its arrival with its cargo sloshing back and forth. Within minutes the entire population of Marla Camp had emerged from their tents, like legions of gophers climbing out of their holes, to watch as we connected the water pump to the huge bladder and began filling it with clean water.

The bladder wasn't perfect, but it was a good temporary solution. And it would have to do until I could figure out what exactly it would take to get someone to drill a well right in the middle of Marla Camp.

As soon as the first folks started topping off their jerricans, the crowd burst into one collective voice, cheering and chanting: *"Moya! Moya! Moya!"*—the Sudanese Arabic word for *water*.

The smile on my face must've been huge that morning as I leaned against the door of my truck, watching the whole scene unfold. And my smile only grew wider as I witnessed what happened next.

The children, having already delivered their day's worth of water back to their families' tents in a matter of minutes versus hiking four hours to the nearest water source, soon realized they now had lots of free time. An impromptu soccer game erupted, the kids using melted plastic trash bags for a ball. Other kids were running around with cars made of sticks and cans and other homemade toys. They were goofing off. Going berserk.

It was the first time I'd ever seen the children of Marla Camp playing . . . playing anything at all.

During that first year in Darfur, I always held close the vision of the children of Marla playing that day. I relied on it to remind me what I was doing there and why I needed to stay on even when all I wanted was to get the hell out of Darfur. It acted as my own personal well to keep me going when times got tough—or whenever people started shooting at me.

From: Libbi Hendley
To: Doc Hendley
Sent: Friday, April 8, 2005, 9:26:16 p.m.
Subject: Phone call

Hi Doc,

I tried to call you over and over today but couldn't get through. If you get a chance to e-mail us that would be great. I know that if I am still a little edgy since hearing about your incident with the Janjaweed then you must be feeling like you're going to jump out of your skin! I am praying that God will be with you and help you work through all that you are feeling and reliving over and over again. Every time I read your letter (and I've read it many, many times) and every time I think or talk about it, the words that God is our shield come to my mind. I am so thankful that He is keeping you safe.

I can't wait to see you again. I hope to talk to you, or hear from you real soon.

I love you,
Mom

TWO

The path that led me to Darfur in 2005 can actually be traced back, believe it or not, to a sleazy old biker bar just outside the tiny town of Sanford, North Carolina.

The bar was part of the old Palomino Motel, a low-slung thirty-dollar-a-night place that catered to folks who'd rent rooms for weeks and months at a time—out-of-town construction workers on local jobs, folks down on their luck, that sort of thing. Anyway, the bar there was called the 19th Hole. I'm pretty sure the name was a ploy to get golfers from the local public golf course to patronize the bar. But it didn't work. Instead, the 19th Hole became a favorite of biker gangs, and any other rowdy redneck folks living or passing through Lee County. And I loved it there. Felt at home.

Much of my life I've felt like I never really fit in anywhere, but something just seemed right at that bar. While most guys my age were partying in frat houses and college bars, I was happiest at the 19th Hole. Of course, there were two big things that spawned my love for the place: (1) I'm crazy for bikes—owned a Harley-Davidson since I was seventeen; and (2) I loved this cute little Italian girl with big brown eyes who tended bar there.

Her name is not important. What is important is that this one girl had me wrapped around her finger so tightly that I spent nearly every spare moment hanging out at the 19th Hole. And I usually wasn't even drinking.

This girl, let's call her Kelly, was a bit of a nutcase with a drinking problem. And I was a drinker with a nutcase problem. By the time she started working at the bar, Kelly had been sober for at least a couple months. So, to support her, I too abstained from alcohol. Every night, I'd sidle up to that sticky horseshoe-shaped bar surrounded with blinking neon beer signs. The dark red carpet was never quite dry, and the place always stank of stale cigarette smoke, but there I'd sit, contentedly sipping on pint after pint of Coca-Cola. I was always hopped up on caffeine and absolutely frothing at the sight of every single beer I'd watch Kelly pour. I wanted to shove my face inside those golden pints and just inhale. But I didn't. I was a supportive boyfriend—and it sucked.

Then, one evening in the spring of 2002, the bar was absolutely slammed. It was a Tuesday, ten-cent-hot-wings night, and the local Pagan's Saints gang had the 19th Hole overflowing with leathers, mullets, and ponytails. I was quietly drinking my Coke when the manager leaned over and asked me if I'd be willing to hop behind the bar and help Kelly out. I'd never tended bar before, but I took to it immediately.

If my parents could see me now . . . I laughed to myself as I slung Natural Light and Jack and Cokes to the hikers. *Damn, they'd be pissed.*

You see, I was raised in one of those perfect families that most people only hear about or see on TV. My dad, he's a gentle-tempered preacher man. Not the fire-and-brimstone type, but the Church has always been a huge part of his life. Mom, also a devout Christian, was a dedicated mother who stayed home to watch after me and my older sister, Kristy, and three brothers, Todd, Bo, and Billy.

My parents named me Dickson, but as a young kid my sister couldn't say my name, so she called me "Dick-Doc." Thank God that name didn't stick. Instead, ever since then my family and friends have simply called me Doc.

When I was growing up we moved around a lot, from Augusta, Georgia, to Chicago to (almost) Africa as missionaries—that's another long story—and back to the South again to Greensboro, North Carolina, where I spent the bulk of my childhood.

While my sister and brothers were deeply committed to

our religious upbringing and my parents' passion for church, I never really drank the Kool-Aid the same way they did, I guess. Sure, I believed in God and went to church on Sundays, and did things like handing out meals with my siblings down at the homeless shelter a couple days a month, which I actually enjoyed, because I felt like we were making a tangible difference.

But still, everyone in my family knew I was different.

I distinctly remember when I was about twelve being on a family trip in Myrtle Beach, South Carolina, with all of us piled into our Chevy Suburban. We were sitting at a stoplight with some gospel station blaring on the radio when a man on a Harley-Davidson rumbled to a stop alongside us. He wore cowboy boots and riding leathers and rode alone. To me, he represented everything cool and independent, and was the total opposite of the people surrounding me in that car. I yearned to become that guy.

I never liked all of the rules that people were tossing at me at church, school, wherever. Rules were stifling. They were for other people. I understood that other people needed those kinds of rules or boundaries, but I saw them as chains that tied me down. And while my brothers and sister, and most kids my age, for that matter, were busy hanging out with friends, going to birthday parties and the mall and crap like that, I was happiest watching old John Wayne westerns or exploring the woods with my BB gun.

My parents were mostly tolerant of my rebellious attitude

(it was pretty harmless, after all), so as a young teenager I was allowed some of the freedom I craved. I camped out in the woods often, and hunted squirrels and rabbits and such. As long as I stayed out of trouble and made it back home in time for church they were fine with me.

Needless to say, being a loner wasn't too good for my social status at school. Actually, I was pretty much an outcast. The popular kids had their group; the nerds even had a clique. But I didn't seem to fit in anywhere. The first time I really had that revelation was in sixth grade during a middle- school dance. I stood there alone in the corner all evening until one girl took pity on me and asked me to dance. It was a mercy dance, though, and that became painfully obvious as she kept looking over her shoulder at her snickering friends while we slowly shuffled back and forth to some Bon Jovi ballad. I felt like a loser. And after that one dance, I retreated to my corner, where I cried. That was a definite low point of growing up.

Naturally, my family never had alcohol in the house. And they certainly didn't approve of any of us kids drinking. Yet I had my first taste of the stuff back in the eighth grade on a school choir field trip. It was whiskey from mini airplane bottles—and I liked it. I kept drinking throughout high school, oftentimes doing it all alone, sipping whiskey or beer around a campfire in the woods. It just seemed like the kind of thing a cowboy or a biker would do.

But still I remained uncool and unnoticed until my second year of high school. I guess that was about the age that some students started thinking that being a loner and a rebel was actually cool. Then I started riding motorcycles when I turned fifteen, and bought my first Harley two years later, which definitely upped my mysterious-loner-guy quotient even higher. I was the rebellious son of a preacher man, with shoulder-length dirty blond hair, and girls started paying attention to me. Soon I was getting dates. Other guys noticed that whatever I was doing—or, rather, what I wasn't doing—started attracting some pretty cute girls. So, all of a sudden, I guess I became kind of cool.

But as it turns out, I was maybe a little too cool for my own good. Before long I had become the life of the party. And if anyone wanted to know where the party was happening, they'd call me. Soon I got wrapped up in maintaining my coolness, and for the first time in my life I was focusing on winning the popularity contest. And it sucked. I liked the guy I was before way more.

Once I graduated high school, I left the popular crowd behind and embraced the biker lifestyle even more. I was drinking harder, hanging with a rough crowd, and I even found my way into the occasional bar fight—usually standing up for a woman who was being harassed or some such (I was just doing my best to be John Wayne on a Harley).

So anyway, me working there in a biker bar serving alcohol to the dregs of Lee County actually made perfect sense. And I was loving every minute of it.

As the weeks went on at the 19th Hole, I realized the folks

I was meeting at that bar, the regulars, were just real people. They didn't blow smoke up my ass or tell me how I should live. They'd simply share their life stories with me. I got to hear about everything, their jobs, their raises, getting fired, getting married, divorced, family dying, all of it. I really enjoyed being a part of their lives. Bartending is counseling at its finest, really—for both them and me. The regulars were a tight-knit group, and, as far as I was concerned, tighter than the folks at any church I'd ever been to in my life. And for the first time I realized that maybe I wasn't destined to be a loner after all.

I tended bar off and on at the 19th Hole for about three months while finishing up the semester at Central Carolina Community College. By that time, Kelly and I were on the rocks (again). And with us both working at the same bar and living in the same tiny town, things were getting a little weird. So I decided to hit the road.

That summer, I bought a 1995 Harley Heritage Softail motorcycle through an old friend of mine who was living in New Zealand at the time. Their dollar was in the crapper, so I was able to afford a way nicer bike than what I could get here in the States. For three hundred bucks he had it shipped to Los Angeles. I took a Greyhound bus out there and rode the Harley all the way back home, the long way. In fact, it took nearly three months.

Winding my way along the most indirect routes I could find, I traveled from L.A. to Ventura to Vegas to Tahoe, up to Reno and on to see the redwoods in northern California, and then to Oregon and Washington and Vancouver. Along the way I'd camp on the side of the road or just crash with local bikers. I rode and drank my way all over the Canadian Rockies, to Banff, Alberta, up to Edmonton, where it was daylight nearly all night long; then I shot back down to Bigfork, Montana—one of my favorite places in the world. Then I did Mount Rushmore, Wyoming, the Badlands of South Dakota, everything. Every morning I'd just wake up, hop on my bike, and say to myself, *This is perfect. I don't have anyplace to be and no particular time to get there.*

It was a trip of a lifetime for me.

For my mom, it was the worst time of her life. She later told me that she was certain when I left North Carolina for Los Angeles that it'd be the last time she'd ever see me. She cried herself to sleep many nights that summer. She thought I'd "lost the plot" for good and that I'd no doubt end up in prison—or dead.

But that wasn't the case. All that time on two wheels actually helped me to heal, to forget about Kelly and some other heavy things in my past I don't even like thinking about.

By the time I made it as far east as Kansas, I started getting bored with just riding and drinking all the time. So I decided to get to Interstate 40 and haul ass back to Raleigh in time to enroll for the new semester at NC State.

I made it to Raleigh around mid-August, after nearly three months on the road. On the way into town I saw that a new bar, Club Mojo, was opening near campus. There was a big white Hiring sign in the window, and the logo, two monkeys beating on a drum, caught my eye. So I stopped.

I roared up and parked my bike on the sidewalk by the front door. I was straight off my road trip and still wearing full riding leathers and boots. My dirty blond hair was just that, dirty. And long. And I hadn't touched my beard in months. It was scraggly and long and stained with road tar. But I strolled inside with the newfound swagger I'd developed on the road.

Club Mojo smelled fresh, like bleach and just-cut limes. The place was newly painted, and red velvet curtains hung along the walls, creased perfectly. I told the general manager I had experience as a bartender and, to my surprise, he hired me on the spot.

I started work two days later. It was a Thursday and Club Mojo was packed. There must've been at least three hundred people there, and the line at the bar was four rows deep. Pumping club music was accompanied by two weird dudes drumming live to the beat (they were the monkeys), all of which made it very tough for me to hear the orders being shouted my way. But truthfully it didn't really matter that I couldn't hear.

I didn't know how to make a mojito, Royal Flush, Sex on the Beach, or any of that crap people were ordering. So I just winged it, started making up drinks and sliding them across the bar. I was pretty sure I had everyone fooled until closing time, when the general manager pulled me aside.

"You've never bartended before, have you, Doc?"

"Yeah, I worked in a biker bar. But I just never had to serve those froofy drinks. It was straight beer, whiskey, and rum, pretty much."

"Well, this is a real bar. And you're a terrible bartender, Doc. You've got one week to figure it out."

I needed that job, and I needed to prove to myself that I could hack this. So I bought a drink recipe book and started cramming. I memorized the most popular drinks, the wacky shots, just enough to get by. And it worked. Club Mojo kept me on, and I eventually became a damn good bartender.

Pretty quickly I realized which drink orders and which patrons I needed to pay most attention to. The people who ordered top-shelf liquor, or drinks like a dirty martini, those were folks who know how their drink was supposed to taste. If I screwed up, they'd be onto it and they'd be pissed. On the other hand, for those ordering the Sex on the Beach or the Fuzzy Navel or some other froofy drink or shot, it was most important that I simply got the color of the drink correct. I realized the people who ordered those types of drinks didn't really know what they were supposed to taste like in the first place. So as long as they tasted good and approximated the color of a tequila sunrise or whatever, I was good to go.

Of course, being a truly good bartender doesn't have all that much to do with how fast and good you are at making a dirty martini. It's more about how good you are at making relationships with the customers. The most important thing is that they have a good time at your bar. That said, all of the above goes out the window when the bar is packed and the line of customers is three rows deep.

At the time I was living in a nearly condemned two-bedroom house with no heat and a window AC unit that roared as loud as my Harley. Everything I owned fit in a single cardboard box. I didn't shower much, wore the same pair of Levi's jeans and white V-neck T-shirt nearly every day—I guess I just still enjoyed being a dirty biker guy. But at work I always took pride in keeping a clean bar—no one wanted to be sticking to the bar or be assaulted by fruit flies swarming the garnish tray.

The nightlife scene in Raleigh was small, and so I quickly got to know bartenders and servers from all the other nearby bars. I also realized that if you take care of other bartenders when they are on your turf, they'll take care of you whenever you're on theirs. I drank way too much and made lots of good friends along the way, but none better than Tasha Craft, a sweet yet sassy twenty-two-year-old brunette who worked across the street at the Flying Saucer. Our relationship started under inauspicious conditions. I was apparently "dating" a friend of hers, whom I'd recently broken it off with, so I was automatically labeled some kind of self-centered prick. But Tasha and I would soon become fast friends.

She was different from all the other girls in that scene. She was carefree, and didn't seem worried about what people thought of her. While other girls were carrying designer purses, Tasha had an olive-drab military surplus satchel she got while doing wildlife conservation work in Africa. She wasn't perfect, and didn't try to be, and that made her beautiful. Tasha was also one of the only people who has ever had the gall to call me out when I was wrong, while still encouraging me and my dreams.

Though I always paid just enough attention to my coursework at NC State to get the bare minimum done, and showed up to class often enough to keep my teachers off my back, my main focus was on a different world—the three tree-lined blocks of bars and nightclubs that made up Glenwood Avenue. I soon moved my way up from Club Mojo to a popular college bar where the tips were better but the crowd was maddening, to the pinnacle of Glenwood: the Hibernian Pub. That cozy authentic Irish pub on the corner of Glenwood and West North Street had a strong crew of regulars and brisk business every single night of the week. I cut my hair, trimmed my beard, put on a tie, and eventually earned the best shifts tending that huge mahogany bar. Hell, I even scored a gig playing guitar and singing every Wednesday night. I was moving up. For me, life was all about the Hibernian and late nights with my new friends. It was like I was the mayor of the block and anything was possible.

But Tasha always kept me grounded.

One Wednesday in the fall of 2003, after I finished playing my last set at the Hibernian, Tasha and I were sharing whiskey at the bar, gearing up for another late night in Raleigh.

"What the hell are you doing, dude?" she asked, after downing a shot.

"What do you mean? I'm sitting here drinking some whiskey with my best friend." I pretended to be puzzled, but knew exactly what she was getting at.

"You know what I mean. You've got one more semester before graduation, which is a frickin' miracle, considering you never go to class. You've got potential, Doc; you can't just hang around Raleigh bartending and playing a few shitty gigs the rest of your life."

"But I don't ever want to work in an office. . . ."

"Look, just because you're getting a degree doesn't mean you have to quit your bartending job and go work in a cubicle. Do what the hell you want to do, just don't settle."

Those words stung, because I knew Tasha was right.

Most nights I just worked at the Hibernian, then stayed up late into the night drinking with friends. It was great. The only problem was that I'd almost always wake up the next morning with a sinking feeling in my stomach, like I should be doing something better with my life. Looking back, I think I was probably feeling guilty about how I was choosing to live my life. I was living selfishly and always for the moment, without anyone else in mind. My world had gotten very small. Like a hangover that haunted me every morning was the feeling that I was wasting my life.

About that time, December 2003, my parents were living west of Raleigh in the little town of Boone, North Carolina, tucked into the Appalachian Mountains. I was planning to head home for the holidays, but before I left, my mom asked if I could do her a favor. A friend had bought a Chihuahua puppy in Raleigh as a Christmas present for her daughter. All I had to do was pick up the dog and deliver it to her friend in Boone. I couldn't think of a lamer way to spend my time, but I agreed to do it for Mom.

Once I had the tiny granola-colored puppy I seriously contemplated strapping its carrier to the backseat of my Harley for the three-hour ride up to the mountains. But a cooler head prevailed, and eventually I settled instead on setting the dog on the bench seat beside me in my old black Ford F-150.

Mom gave me directions to the lady's house. She lived a way out from my parents' home, and I was hoping I could quickly drop the dog off and still make it home in time for dinner.

As my truck's tires spit driveway gravel into the chilly evening air, I was busy planning my excuse about why I had to drop the dog and run. But much to my surprise, my mom's friend was actually a really interesting woman. Though she seemed a little too inquisitive about what I planned to do after college—my mom probably put her up to it—once she began telling me about her husband's role at an international aid organization called Samaritan's Purse, I completely forgot that I'd been planning a quick escape. It sounded like an amazing job, flying around the world doing humanitarian work in developing countries. He had adventure, danger,

excitement, everything, and most important, he was helping people along the way. It made my world bartending in
Raleigh seem totally inconsequential and a bit lame. It also
sparked some fond memories of how much I had enjoyed
helping the homeless and doing other service projects with
my sister and brothers back home.

Now, I'm no expert in how the subconscious mind works,
and it could've simply been the whiskey, or the conversation
I had earlier that day, or divine inspiration, or all of it mashed
together, but later that same night I sat bolt upright in bed
with a string of words spinning around my brain.

Wine.

Water.

Wine and water.

Wine to water.

"Funny, that's backward," I thought. Obviously I was
familiar with the story of Jesus changing the water to wine,
because I'd heard my dad preach on it many times. It was actually my favorite. The way I saw it, that story proved Jesus was
a way cooler dude than what all the churchy folk back home
had taught me.

But what did it mean? I asked myself, *What? Is there something about water? I don't understand.*

My mind was racing. I was tossing and turning.

Backward or not, it was definitely a catchy phrase, I thought
as I peeled back the covers on my bed and stood up. I grabbed
a pen and paper off my bedside table and wrote it down.

Wine to water.

Then I went to the computer and started Googling. Up until that point I was ignorant about the world's water crisis—didn't even know that one existed.

What I was reading startled me. It couldn't be true. I was just learning to use the Internet, so I wasn't totally confident that what I was reading was accurate. . . . Unclean water kills a child every twenty seconds—it's more lethal than AIDS, malaria, and tuberculosis combined. One in every six people on our planet has no access to clean water—that's over a billion folks. In many developing countries, like Sudan, Ethiopia, Uganda, India, and Cambodia, women and children have to walk as many as four to five hours each day to gather water. And once they get it, it's often dirty enough to cause members of their family to die. The details were dizzying.

The more articles I read, the more I realized these stats and figures were indeed true. There was a tight knot growing in my stomach. How come I'd never heard about this before? Why wasn't anyone doing something to fix this?

Then something happened. Those words, *wine to water*, all started making sense. I decided right then and there, *There's no sense in just getting worked up about it unless I do something to really fight it.* Once I learned the hard truth about the world's water crisis I really had no choice. I had to help.

I stayed up all night researching and sketching out the concept for what would eventually become my nonprofit, Wine to Water. Deep down I think I had been yearning for a way out of the rut I was drinking myself into in Raleigh. The thought of somehow being able to one day serve people who were desperate for help felt right to me. I had been feeling guilty about where my life was headed, and in a way this seemed like an opportunity to start making up for some of the stupid, selfish things I'd been doing for the past handful of years.

I called Tasha the very next morning. I was yearning to tell her, to tell anyone, about my new plan. From all those years working at bars, it dawned on me that our regulars and patrons were mostly good people who cared about the world around them and would happily do their part to make a difference. They just didn't know how or where to start. I'd simply throw a party at a local bar to benefit the world's water crisis, and they could have fun while helping others in need.

"Hell, yeah, Doc, where do I sign up to help?" said Tasha. "It's about time you used your head for something other than drinking whiskey and singing Johnny Cash."

And with that, together Tasha and I put the first Wine to Water event into motion. I began spending less time pounding beers at the bars and instead channeled my free time and energy into this project. Neither I nor Tasha had any experience planning an event like this; we simply used the contacts we'd developed locally in the bartending world.

I contacted a friend who ran a big nightclub in Raleigh, the Office, and got him to donate the space on a Wednesday, a night he'd normally be closed. Tasha hooked up some free cases of wine through a distributor, while I scored a few kegs from the local Anheuser-Busch folks. We got a friend to agree to deejay late-night, and I'd play live music for the early crowd. We settled on a date about a month out, February 4, 2004, and bam!—Wine to Water was a reality.

Tasha and I were both nervous that night, but the event went off better than we could've expected.

More than three hundred people showed up, easily filling the Office's bar, dance floor, and VIP lounge. It was a good crowd. Early in the night, lots of my friends and family came. Even my parents and some of their church friends drove down from Boone to be a part of the event. By late evening, the crowd had grown larger and louder as all of my bar friends and the local service industry folks showed up.

The whole event happened really organically. People were simply having fun and donating money to a good cause. I didn't have to hard-sell anyone. I just stood up and gave a quick twenty-second speech.

"Look, folks, we're here tonight because I've learned about this global water crisis, and it's scary stuff. Over a billion people in this world don't have access to clean water. And I think we need to do something about it. All the money you guys donate tonight will go directly to fighting for clean water for these folks. Just by y'all being here and enjoying life, we can help make a difference."

By the end of the night, after the doors were closed, Tasha and I sat together at the bar drinking a couple pints and counting all the money we'd raised in the tip jars and at the door. I couldn't help feeling like a drug dealer or a mafioso as I gripped several thick stacks of money, more than six thousand dollars in all.

"Man, we're going to be able to help a lot of people with all this cash," I said to Tasha, giggling like a kid. "Now we've just got to figure out how in the hell to get it to the people who need it."

We raised a lot more money than Tasha and I had expected. And what was crazy was that earlier the same night, the owner of a local dive bar called the Comet approached me and asked if we'd host a Wine to Water event at his bar later in the month too. So we did, and we raised another six thousand dollars without much trouble. Other people who'd just heard about the events even began mailing in donations.

This could actually really work, I thought to myself. *This is only one city, in one state, in one part of our country. What if this Wine to Water thing ever really caught on?*

THREE

I t was one of those early spring evenings when the day is warm but the night comes on quickly and with a chill. I was working the happy-hour shift at the Hibernian, and we still had our big floor-to-ceiling roll-up windows open from that afternoon, so the cool night was really starting to seep into the bar.

I enjoyed stealing a glance or two at the cute office girls, all done up and in heels, clip-clopping along Glenwood past those big windows of ours on their way home every evening. And it was good to see that some of them had finally traded in their wool slacks for spring skirts. *Thank you, Lord.*

I laughed to myself while making smooth circles with my cleaning rag on the big mahogany bar.

About that time, Matt, one of my favorite regulars, slid onto the stool in front of me. He was a prominent local businessman, forever in a suit and tie, and he stopped by most days for happy hour on his way home from the office.

"Doc."

"Good evening, sir," I said, methodically placing a white bar napkin in front of him, then a Miller Lite bottle—Matt's usual.

"So, how's the old fund-raising coming, Doc?"

"It's actually going great, Matt. I've been really surprised at how much everyone is getting behind me on this."

"I'm not surprised," said Matt, after taking a long sip of Miller Lite "You know, Doc, we all believe in you, man, and this noble cause you've decided to go after."

"That means a lot, Matt."

"But, please, just promise me one thing," he said, looking me straight in the eyes. "Make sure you guys use that money you've raised in a way that will make us all proud."

"Of course, Matt. You can count on it."

I had been drinking less, feeling better about myself, and spending more and more of my time on Wine to Water. And I was really starting to stress out about the money. And Matt's request knocked it home for me—made it personal and even more urgent. Tasha and I had done a great job of putting on the two Wine to Water events and raising the donations. But we still hadn't figured out exactly how and where to put those donations to work. And Tasha had jetted to Australia on a whim a couple weeks earlier for a two-month "sabbatical," as she called it. So now it was totally on me to make the right decision with this money.

I never wanted Wine to Water to be like one of those bullshit nonprofits I'd heard about on the news that used the majority of the donations to pay staff and run their businesses while little of it actually ever made it to the people who needed it most. I wasn't going to let that happen. I didn't know exactly how it was going to work out, but I'd figure it out.

It was in early May, on the three-hour drive up the mountains to Boone, where I'd been spending more of my time to pull myself away from the craziness and late-night lifestyle back in Raleigh, that the answer—or at least part of it—came to me. As the rolling green hills, tobacco farms, and weathered red barns passed by, I realized that it was pointless for me to try to reinvent the wheel. There was no way that I'd personally be able to take the money to some foreign country and expect to do anything meaningful with it. First off, I'd probably spend half of it just flying there, and then I'd waste the other half trying to figure out how to use it to help these folks get clean water. I needed to donate it to an established, trustworthy nonprofit that was already doing good water work.

That was when I remembered the lady and the Chihuahua.

My mom gave her friend a call, and by the following Monday I had an appointment to meet with a man from Samaritan's Purse, a huge and well-respected international aid organization based nearby in Boone. His name was Ken Isaacs, and apparently he'd started as a well driller; gone on to operate the organization's water programs, working in the field throughout Africa for twenty years; and eventually moved his way up the ranks to become director of all of Samaritan's Purse's international projects.

Prepping for my meeting, I had read that Samaritan's Purse maintained a better than 90-percent-to-10-percent projects-to-administrative ratio with their donations, meaning nearly all the money went straight to the people in need. But before I'd turn over our Wine to Water money, I was going to insist that Isaacs first assured me that it would go directly to water-specific programs in the field.

As I walked into his high-ceilinged office, I was overwhelmed. Everywhere there were photographs of Isaacs working on wells, hanging out in the desert with rebel soldiers, and shaking hands with tribal leaders. One wall was covered in old weapons—a World War I rifle, tribal African swords and carved wooden shields, small knives and rusty daggers. On the opposite wall hung official-looking letters and proclamations. As I waited there for Isaacs to arrive, one letter in particular caught my eye. It was a handwritten note on official White House stationery from then-president

George W. Bush, personally thanking Isaacs for all the work he'd done over the years.

Holy shit, I thought to myself, as I nervously rubbed my clammy hands on my blue jeans. *This guy is big-time.*

Just then, Isaacs opened the door and walked briskly to his big leather chair. He was a tall, thin fellow with a bald head and a bushy, grayish-brown beard. He wore a tie and shiny black shoes. As Isaacs leaned over the wide desk to shake my hand, he smiled warmly. But I felt his gaze fall upon the tattoos sprouting beneath my sleeves. I suddenly felt self-conscious, like I didn't belong here. And I was nervous. Rarely do I ever have trouble talking with people, but this was one of those times.

Isaacs quickly dived into the meeting. In a very matter-of-fact, purposeful manner, he began asking me about Wine to Water. I stammered a bit while explaining to him how Tasha and I had raised the money we were considering donating to him. Of course, judging from the evidence on his office walls, I knew our donation would actually be small beans to this man. But if it was, he never let me know it.

Instead Isaacs embraced my raw passion, and my insistence that the Wine to Water funds be used fairly and appropriately.

"Okay, Doc, what's the deal? Why are you really doing all this?"

"I . . . I don't know exactly," I said, stumbling over my words. "I guess it's just important to me."

"What's important to you?" he fired back.

"I just recently learned about the world's water crisis and I feel like I need to do something about it. And I guess I'm also trying to do something different with my life."

I originally expected this meeting to be about my learning more about Samaritan's Purse and how our donations could be put to good use. But instead, Isaacs deftly morphed the conversation into an interview about me. He wanted to know what I was studying in college and how soon I'd complete my degree.

"All right, I'll tell you what, Doc. When you're finished with school, why don't you come work for me? We'll send you wherever you want in the world and you can learn about water work firsthand."

I looked at Isaacs, but my gaze shot right through him. I was dumbfounded.

"Listen, you keep your Wine to Water money and just go and see for yourself," he added. "That way you can support the programs you want to support, maybe even some of the ones you're doing there in the field for us."

I was shocked. I wasn't expecting this at all.

"So, what do you say, Doc?"

"Yeah, that would be awesome," I said.

"I think you need to know what it's like in the field. You need to know what's really happening out there. So where do you think you would like to go?"

Again, I was lost. I had no idea. If he'd asked me to name five developing countries, I probably couldn't have even done that, much less pick a place for myself to work on water projects.

"I don't know. How about you send me to where I'm most needed? Just send me to the worst place in the world."

"Seriously?"

"Yeah.

Isaacs paused. He was obviously thinking.

"Okay, well, that designation would fall on either Afghanistan or Darfur. We already have teams in place in Afghanistan, but none in Darfur."

"All right," I said.

"There's a huge need in Darfur right now. I haven't been there, and neither has anyone else in my organization, so you'll be one of the first people on the ground there. It'll be interesting and potentially pretty dangerous, but you'll be able to see how things work from the ground up."

"Okay, that sounds good," I said, kind of not believing those words had just left my mouth.

"Excellent. Someone from my office will be in touch with more info, and we'll get you started in August."

I walked slowly through the parking lot and straddled my Harley. My mind was spinning. It all happened so quickly.

"Did I really just get a job?" I asked out loud, as if someone would actually answer.

From: Doc Hendley
To: Tasha Craft
Sent: Sunday, May 7, 2004, 1:17:56 p.m.
Subject: Yo

How's Australia? I hear you're hopping from island to island on some little broke-ass boat that you bought down there. Sounds like you're living like a queen!

Guess what!?!? You're never going to believe this. I just got out of a meeting with this guy from Samaritan's Purse. And instead of us talking about sending all our Wine to Water money to their water programs, he offered me a job working for them overseas! He told me I could then use our money to help fund whatever water project I was working on! I'm leaving after I finish school this summer to a place in Africa called Darfur. I don't know much about the place but from what I hear it's pretty bad there. I'm in complete shock right now and chomping at the bit to get out of here. I wish I could just leave now.

Tasha, thank you so much for everything, for all your help with Wine to Water, and for encouraging me to do something more with my life than just pour drinks and play shitty music.

I've already left Raleigh to take my last class in Boone and spend the next couple months with my family before I leave for Darfur. So when you get back from

Down Under you need to come hang with me before I take off.

Take care darlin',
Doc

As soon as I had the chance, I hopped on the computer and started researching Darfur. The first thing that popped on the screen was a photograph of a mother and daughter covered head to toe in dirty yet colorful clothing. They were standing beside a makeshift tent, and their faces were blank, emotionless. It looked really windy, because their clothes were flowing and the plastic sheeting of their tent snapped in the breeze. I'm not sure what captivated me more, the faces, their living conditions, or the empty desert landscape that surrounded them.

Clicking on more photos with my mouse, I realized that the background in every picture was either a sandy, windblown desert or dry, cracked earth with mean-looking thornbushes and sparse trees scattered about. I wondered how those plants managed to survive in such a harsh environment, much less the people. Then I saw a picture with the word *Janjaweed* in the caption. *What in the world is a Janjaweed?* I thought to myself.

I clicked on more and more links, revealing more and more photos of a windswept, sand-covered place. There were endless photos of armed men on camels, decimated villages still smoldering, boy soldiers carrying AK-47s, and makeshift tent cities and ragged refugees, mostly women and children, lined up for food and water.

From what I could see, Darfur didn't look like much fun. Then I dug in and started reading the news stories. It was shocking stuff. The situation in Darfur was complex and volatile.

Darfur is a region about the size of France on the western side of Sudan, Africa's largest country. It's a semiarid place with a population of about six million. The vast majority are black Africans who are subsistence farmers and peasants, while the minority are Arab nomadic herders. For generations these two groups have fought over land and water rights. The black Africans want to work the land and grow crops, while the Arabs feel they are free to roam and herd their animals wherever they'd like, traveling up and down the region following the rainy seasons and growing seasons. But whenever the rainfall dwindled and food and water became tougher to come by, the conflict between the two groups grew worse. Eventually, each side organized its own rebel forces—the black Africans created the Sudanese Liberation Army (SLA) and the Justice and Equality Movement (JEM) to fight the Arab tribesmen known as the Janjaweed, which in the local dialect means *evil horseman*. Despite what many have mistakenly assumed, this was never a religious battle, as both groups are predominantly Muslim. It was a struggle for land and resources, pure and simple.

This conflict continued to rage for decades. Meanwhile, around the late 1980s and 1990s, the black African people of the Darfur region began feeling as though they weren't being fairly represented in the Sudanese government, which was headed by President Omar al-Bashir, an Arab and former Sudanese military leader who came to power in 1989 as part of a military coup. The Darfuris' feelings of unrest and underrepresentation finally came to a head in February 2003, when the SLA and JEM began attacking Sudanese government targets. Al-Bashir was getting nervous that they might eventually serve him a little of his own medicine (in the form of a coup), so he had a grand idea. Since the Janjaweed were already fighting against the black Africans, al-Bashir decided to enlist their help, quietly arming and training the Janjaweed rebels and aligning them with the Sudanese government army to quell the black African uprising. Of course, the government publically denied any involvement with the Janjaweed.

The two quickly grew to become a formidable team, unleashing terror on the black Africans. And not just the rebel groups. Their violence was wholesale, terrorizing the general population. Working secretly, but in concert with the Sudanese military, the Janjaweed were conducting a full-fledged genocide against the black African Sudanese people. There were stories of the military using helicopter gunships to destroy villages, then calling in the Janjaweed by Thuraya sat phones, who would ride in on camels to finish the job, indiscriminately killing villagers, gang-raping the women, and burning the villages to the ground.

From 2003 to 2004, it's estimated that more than a hundred thousand civilians were killed by the Janjaweed and the government of Sudan, while more than a million others had been displaced from their villages, fleeing in fear to massive tent cities. And this was exactly where the government wanted the black Africans, because, thanks to the poor living conditions and unclean water in those camps, hundreds of thousands more black Africans continued to die.

About that time the rest of the world started taking notice of the genocide, and international aid organizations, including Samaritan's Purse, slowly began arriving to help care for the legions of displaced Darfuris.

From: Terry Harmon, Samaritan's Purse
To: Doc Hendley
Sent: Tuesday, July 27, 2004, 6:40:17 p.m.
Subject: Darfur information

I know you probably have some questions about what we will be doing in Darfur and what the conditions are like. You've probably seen TV news reports about the crisis in Darfur. It is a refugee situation where people have run for their lives. More than one million people are displaced.

As for living conditions, Ken Isaacs wrote the following to me earlier today:

It is in the middle of the Sahara desert in one of the most remote areas of the world. The living conditions will be horrible. It is rainy now. When that is over it will be over 125 degrees in the days. Travel is hard. Water is little. Anyone that is serious about going will be able to look on the net or on TV and see the conditions. There is no way to give more specifics but this location cannot be candy-coated.

Attached below is a list of potential preparation/packing suggestions that was forwarded to me earlier today.

That is all I know at this point. I'm sorry I don't have more specifics to share with you. If you have questions, please let me know and I will try to get answers for you.

Terry
Terry L. Harmon
Field Staff Coordinator
Projects Department
Samaritan's Purse

I continued reading and learning about the crisis in Darfur. I realized I could be killed over there, but I wasn't really scared. It was partly because I was naive, unaware of exactly what I was about to experience, and honestly, I felt like I had gotten myself into (and out of) some pretty crazy situations over the past few years working in bars and living the biker lifestyle. I was young and a little bit reckless, and I guess I figured there wasn't much that could surprise or scare me anymore. I had fought in my fair share of bar brawls, had my head cracked on the pavement, even got a gun pulled on me by some crazy drug dealer. I was probably much closer to death while living and partying in Raleigh, whether it would be from getting killed by some angry drug dealer or drinking myself to death. Deep down, I think I also felt like, since I was headed to Darfur to do the right thing, to help people who really needed help, maybe God would watch over me and smile for once.

I was ready to go. Naturally my family was nervous for me, and my favorite uncle, John from Montana, even begged me not to go.

"You don't understand that Muslim culture, Doc. And what are you going to gain by going over there? It's a noble cause, but it's not worth losing your life over this stuff."

But I can honestly say I never once considered backing out. In fact, in the weeks leading up to my departure I grew increasingly restless. I couldn't stand not being there. It was the unknown that was freaking me out and the waiting that was killing me.

On August 31, 2004, my parents dropped me off in Raleigh, and, alone, I boarded a plane bound for Kharthoum International Airport, Sudan.

FOUR

From: Doc Hendley
To: Jeff Hendley
Sent: Monday, September 6, 2004, 2:45:21 p.m.
Subject: First day in Sudan

howdy pops. i'm gonna keep this short, 'cause the
keyboard is in arabic.

I can't describe this place in words for y'all to understand. It looks like world war three just hit. There are
toppled buildings everywhere and piles of rubble all
along the so-called roads. I am beginning to understand

all the mess behind the red tape. I have no power. I am at the disposal of whichever sudanese official is in charge that day. It is already a very humbling experience.

There are hardly any driving rules, except watch out for the carts pulled by donkeys and watch out for the crowd that constantly seems to wander into the road. And the occasional runaway goat. I'm already finding out that i'm gonna have to learn arabic in order to get anything done. So i'll scrap what little spanish i know for now and work on one that i can't even read.

Nyala (nee-a-la) is where i'm headed next. That is where i'll be for good. There is one railroad into town that brings food supplies and gas every two weeks for the whole town. The janjaweed militia is based not too far southeast of nyala and the railroad is a constant war zone with them and the darfur rebels to the north. So, many times nyala has to go without gas food and power depending on the attacks around the railroad. That is around the area where a dozen aid workers were supposedly kidnapped not too long ago by the janjaweed.

I wish i could write more, but i have to head off and try and get permission from the sudanese police to go to nyala. Security is real tight here for going to darfur, but once you get there it seems that security is almost nonexistent.

I don't know if i'll be able to write again, but i'll try before i head into darfur.

Love,

Doc

For five days, I waited. I was in the capital of Khartoum spinning my wheels (both literally and figuratively) as I toured the city on a motorcycle I borrowed from the Samaritan's Purse offices, while also waiting for the Sudanese government to allow me to enter Darfur. I was excited to get on the ground and start my work, but first I needed the official paperwork from the government's Humanitarian Aid Commission, a.k.a. HAC. Turns out, the acronym is pretty dang fitting, as HACK—sorry, I mean HAC—was notoriously slow and challenging to deal with.

I was hoping to make it to Nyala, a small end-of-the-road town in the northern half of southern Darfur some five hundred miles southwest of Khartoum. It was the terminus for both the regional railway and the main road, and my eventual home base for the next twelve months.

Finally I got my paperwork in hand and, at about nine a.m. on a bright September day, I shuffled aboard a twin-engine prop airplane operated by Mid Airlines (which we'd later nickname Midair Collision due to the consensus among my fellow field staff that the airline's planes were a bit dodgy).

The small plane I boarded was definitely older than what I was accustomed to flying on. Inside, the seats were threadbare with cigarette ashtrays still in the armrests; lengths of tape seemingly held pieces of the interior together, while loose panels hung from the ceiling, swinging as the plane taxied down the runway.

I might've been more concerned for my safety had those feelings not been eclipsed by my overwhelming concern that I looked like a dweeb. I was the only Caucasian person among the dozen or so passengers (the plane was only half-full), and instead of my normal uniform of blue jeans, black biker boots, and a white Hanes V-neck tee, I was wearing what might as well have been a clown suit.

I had been very concerned about the extreme temperatures I'd encounter in Darfur, so my mom sewed me a poncho-style shirt from some lightweight material she bought at Walmart. It was a flowing, loose-fitting shirt with the neck embroidered with a faux African tribal pattern. I wore it with lightweight slacks and Teva sandals with a similar African tribal pattern on the Velcro straps. I had also grown my blond beard out so it was long, and in an effort to blend in, I'd dyed it black with a box of Just for Men hair dye.

I looked ridiculous.

Under my poncho, I wore a hand-sewn deerskin pouch slung across my bare chest. A Native American man from Boone made it for me to carry my passport and cash. To complete my alien look, I was carrying a mini travel guitar and a bright blue Kelty backpack jammed with all of my gear for the year.

I was completely uncomfortable in my own skin. These were clothes I'd never have worn in my real life back home. So why the hell was I wearing them now, on one of the most important journeys of my life?

As the plane took off from Khartoum, I peered through my tiny porthole of a window and watched as the city slowly disappeared. The last thing I could make out was a spot near Khartoum where the mighty White Nile River and the Blue Nile converge.

Soon, desert was all I could see in every direction. No roads. No huts. It was all red dirt, without a sign of life. I figured this was what the surface of Mars must look like. *There's no way anybody could live down there,* I thought. Khartoum was bad, but holy crap if it wasn't getting worse. I was flying over hell itself.

For hours red dirt dominated my view; then, occasionally, I'd spot spidery white veins tracing their way through the barren landscape. These were wadis, or dry riverbeds. Later I'd learn that when it does rain, those wadis are transformed into dangerous wild torrents, slurping up trucks and people and livestock.

The only green I could make out from the air was occasional tiny dots of olive-colored brush growing alongside the wadis. The closer we got to Darfur, the greener it became, but that's all relative, of course. Any way you slice it, this was the archetypical desert. And it reminded me a lot of my cross-country motorcycle adventure when I rode through Death Valley, Nevada. There was nothing there, really, except for the occasional passing car and a few gas stations. I remember looking at a digital thermometer on a roadside sign that read a hundred and twenty degrees. That was the first time I'd ever experienced true desert heat. Still, nothing could have really prepared me for the way the oppressive Saharan heat enveloped my body as I walked off that plane and into the oven that is Darfur.

A pair of Samaritan's Purse employees greeted me at the airport and drove me to our compound in the heart of Nyala. The dirt streets were arranged in rough grids, and nearly every building looked the same—all single-story, built with cement block covered in plaster that was the exact same color beige as the dirt streets. It looked as if the desert had simply grown walls.

The only contrast in this drab landscape was the colorful trash strewn about the streets, and the jagged shards of green and brown broken glass lining the ten-foot-high walls that surrounded most of the buildings.

There were people swarming all over the streets, all wearing traditional flowing jellabiyas. Most seemed like they were either coming from or going to the local market. We passed a pair of men shepherding at least two dozen cows across the street, and had a couple close calls along the way, including near misses with a young boy driving a wooden donkey cart, and a tuk tuk, a three-wheeled motorcycle rickshaw. People were literally walking and driving all over the place—no lanes, no road signs to follow. But somehow they were getting where they needed to go. It was something like organized chaos.

I didn't talk much on that ride. Instead I just sucked it all in. I was really in Sudan now, and it was starting to sink in that this was where I'd be living for the next year or so.

Once I arrived at my compound, the pair of large faded yellow metal doors groaned as I swung them open to reveal a small sunny courtyard, an outdoor kitchen, a shower, five simple bedrooms, a big lime tree, and a couple of outhouses—this was my new home.

I had always envisioned that I'd hit the ground running in Darfur, instantly morphing into some superhero water savior—fixing a well with one hand while cradling an orphaned baby in the other. But it didn't happen quite like that.

Truthfully, water work wasn't even on the radar. For the first several weeks, my time was spent solely with logistics. Together with three other young aid workers I began the tedium of establishing a field office for Samaritan's Purse from scratch. We had to shop in the local market, called a souk, for office furniture and beds and chairs and fans for our empty shell of a compound. We needed lots of fans to keep the flies off us and to blow the putrid smell of burning garbage away from our noses—our compound was conveniently located near the local dump. We also had to rent trucks and hire security guards to protect our compound, and hook up our phones, computers, everything. Everything was a process. You have to figure out where you're going to work and how you're going to work before you can actually do any work.

One of the first and most important things I accomplished on the ground in Darfur was changing back into my blue jeans, white T-shirt, and boots. And immediately I felt much better. Sure, it was hot as hell. But I quickly realized I was going to be hot no matter what I wore. And this was the seed of an important realization I'd eventually make: There's a time and a place for trying to blend in, for trying to be culturally sensitive. But, bottom line—you're not a local. You're not an SLA soldier. It's key to stay true to your own personality or you'll risk looking like a kook every time.

Once we got everything set up, there was still lots of downtime those first few weeks as we tried to navigate our way through the local aid landscape. I was getting restless. I'd go to bed every night pissed. *I didn't do shit today!* I'd say to myself. *I just sat around in a hot-ass desert. I've been here for weeks and I haven't saved anybody.*

From: Doc Hendley
To: Jeff Hendley
Sent: Saturday, September 11, 2004, 5:03:54 p.m.
Subject: From Sudan

Pops,

I've been getting a lot of random messages from people who I didn't even know were receiving my e-mail updates. They all are wanting to be added to some sort of mailing list. Will you help me set up some kind of system so that we can send out group e-mails to family and friends, and all the folks out there supporting Wine to Water? If it's cool I'll just send group e-mails like this one to you and then you can forward them on. Thanks, dad!

Hello from Sudan,

I wasn't planning on writing for a while—one because this computer is extremely slow and two because I wanted to wait until the team had some exciting achievement that I can write about. But I felt the need to write about an event that took place this evening that is far from an achievement.

I left Khartoum this week and I have been in Nyala, which is in southern Darfur, for a couple of days now.

things are obviously a lot more on edge here. The first
day I got here the team told me that a guy from an NGO
(another word for aid organization) was shot leaving nyala
heading to a camp northwest of here. his truck was shot
up and a bullet went through the door and both of his
legs. Today, my co-worker matt and i were in the truck
when machine gun fire spit out right near our vehicle.
I'm pretty positive whoever it was wasn't shooting at us
though . . . so don't worry. But the most heart-wrenching
thing happened this evening at dinner. . . .

We have been eating mostly "home cooked" meals,
i.e. camping food, since i've been here. So, tonight we
decided to treat ourselves, after a hard day's work, to
some food in nyala. There is one "restaurant" in the
whole town, which consists of a few plastic chairs and
tables out on a dirt street, and a big metal trash can type
thing where they boil whole chickens for the main dish.
they have a few other "apps" like some sort of potatoes
that looked like corned beef hash, and some fried stuff
called Fasha. Oh yeah, and there is no silverware so we
eat everything including the mushy stuff with our hands.
after arguing about how much we were going to order we
finally ordered and began devouring our two chickens,
hash, fasha, bread, and the other stuff they brought . . .
there's four of us right now by the way.

Anyway, when we were close to being finished a boy
around 15 walked up from the dirt road and began to

stare at our table. He stood there for a few minutes and then slowly began to come closer, mumbling something under his breath. a couple of the restaurant workers rushed to him and tried to shoo him away, but the boy wouldn't leave. it wasn't until I saw tears well up in the boy's eyes, as he focused on our chicken bones, that I knew exactly what was going on. the boy was hungry. Not hungry like we get if we skip lunch, but the type of hunger that drives out all other pain from one's mind and body.

I felt sick. Especially after I noticed all the other children on the corners of the mock street and knew that they were probably just as hungry as this other boy, and the worst thing is . . . I could do nothing. Yeah I could have sat the first boy down and bought him a meal, but what about the other children? What about the 100,000 people within a couple of kilometers from me who have nothing? What about the 200,000 people that fled over the border who've lost everything? What about the 2 million left who aren't lucky enough to have made it across the border, who fear being raped or killed every night, and also have nothing? The sudden realization of what I'm getting myself into hit me like I ton of *#@$ing bricks tonight.

And you know what I can't get out of my head??? You know the one thing that haunts me??? It's that age old phrase that we have all heard from our mothers or fathers, that we all now mock: "Eat the rest of your food, son, because there are starving people over there in Africa."

Tonight I decided to write about a failure. My failure, my team's failure, the church's failure, hell, the whole world's failure. Why is this a failure??? because we have gotten so good at shutting out the things that are uncomfortable. We are masters at ignoring the things that might take us out of our comfort zone. We think that if we just finish our plate then we'll be doing the starving people in this world some sort of favor.

Whoa, sorry about that. I think I just blacked out. Anyway, thank you all for your prayers. We need them, but please, please pray for these people, they need prayers far more than me or my team. because in the end we all are "sure of what we hope for and certain of what we do not see."

peace out yo,
doc

p. s. *please* write me e-mails, I won't be able to reply to all of them swiftly because the internet here is weird, but It is easier to receive e-mails and I really love reading them at night. So please continue to write me, even if it is just a funny joke or something, thanks

. . .

One of the most valuable things I learned that first month about working in the humanitarian aid world is this: You can't expect to make things happen overnight.

Eventually I decided to quit beating myself up for not saving people right off the bat, and to instead start immersing myself in the aid world. There was so much to learn. I attended every one of the daily Office for the Coordination of Humanitarian Affairs (OCHA) meetings or security briefings I could. Everyone in those meetings appeared so buttoned-up and experienced. And they all seemed to be speaking in code, using three-letter words like NGOs, IDPs, and NFIs. It took sitting through a handful of meetings before I finally figured out what these folks were talking about. I also began volunteering with other aid organizations to help with whatever missions they had going. I'd do whatever, whenever, partnering with whomever needed help.

One week I'd be handing out NFIs (that's nonfood items) like plastic sheeting, soap, and white UNICEF jerricans for carrying water to the nearly twelve thousand IDPs (internally displaced persons) who had sought shelter from the Janjaweed violence by fleeing to a new unnamed camp just a couple miles outside of Nyala. Next I helped with the food drops, distributing a month's worth of meals to a stadium-size crowd within just a day and a half. I worked security at those food drops, learning to secure a perimeter around the drop zone. You see, when you've got tens of thousands of hungry people coming to get a month's worth of food, things can get pretty hairy. I also learned how to register households to ensure that all of the food went to the people who needed it most. The most valuable lesson was that men should never be considered the head of a household. There are a couple reasons for this. First, some Darfuri men have multiple wives and, thus, multiple families, so it can be very difficult to track which of their families have been served. Second, and more important, mothers will always do what's in the best interest of their children, while unfortunately some men will sell their aid food in the souk for booze or blow it on gambling.

While food drops weren't exactly the type of work I had signed up to do, I was happy to finally be doing something meaningful with my time. And I loved it, because I was gaining tons of new knowledge. Back home in the States, I never felt truly engaged with the learning in school, but this was something very different. And it turned out to be the perfect education for preparing me to operate an aid organization of my own, because I was being exposed to every part of running and sustaining life in these camps, from accessing water and sanitation to supplying shelter needs and NFIs to distributing food.

After more than a month of learning about all these different aspects, I started to feel really comfortable in my work. I was finally making some sense of the inner workings of the aid world and the politics that must be navigated among multiple organizations in order to get things done, and I had even begun to understand and speak a little Arabic.

About that time I started to feel it—it was finally time. So I contacted Ken Isaacs back in Boone and told him I was ready to begin my water work and to put the Wine to Water donations to good use. Isaacs gave me his blessing, and I never looked back.

That very afternoon, I wrote up a little sign in big black letters on white paper.

HIRING

LOOKING TO HIRE TWO WATER AND SANITATION TECHNICIANS.

PLEASE BRING YOUR CV BY TOMORROW. WILL BE ACCEPTING CVS ALL DAY.

I wrote it in English because I wanted to hire only those who could speak and read English. For starters, I planned on hiring just two local workers (called nationals in the aid world) to help get my water work up and running. As I taped my sign to the front door of our compound, I had no idea what sort of response to expect and whether anyone would even show up at all.

The next morning I woke to commotion outside the walls of our compound. I rolled over and pulled the pillow atop my head, but I could still hear men talking and arguing in Arabic. As I poured my morning coffee the din only grew louder, so I slipped open the peephole on our big metal door and took a look.

It wasn't even seven a.m. and already there were more than fifty men crowding around my little hiring sign. They were rustling about as they jockeyed for position.

"Okay, folks," I said, cracking the door wider. The crowd surged forward. "Form a line! Have your CVs ready. I'll be accepting them in a few minutes."

I watched as the men twisted and turned into a rough queue. I wanted to see how they operated in crowds—who pushed to the front, and who was pushed to the back of the line. One man in particular stood out for me. He was a thin man in his early sixties, probably six feet tall, with short gray hair and scruffy stubble. He was distinguished-looking, but his clothes, a shabby light-colored button-down shirt and khakis, were threadbare.

Some of the men's CVs were well organized, cleanly printed from a computer, while others were handwritten on torn-out pages of notebook paper. As they handed me their CVs, most stood proudly, looking me in the eyes and shaking my hand. But I found my gaze stolen by that older man who was now busy helping another younger, short bald man. It was obvious he was translating the guy's CV into English for him. Soon it was his turn to reach the front of the line.

"Very nice to meet you, sir," the tall gentleman said to me as he confidently handed over his own CV. "My name is Hilary Dimo."

"Nice to meet you, Mr. Dimo," I said.

The paper said he spoke seven languages, from English to Dinka to Fur to Swahili. He was a Christian and a university graduate. And he would later become my right-hand man in Darfur.

Near the end of the line was Amir, the younger bald man Hilary had been helping. While it was obvious that Hilary knew his stuff and would be a great asset, what struck me about Amir was how subservient he was. The others treated him badly, pushing him to the back of the line, kicking him around like some stray dog. He spoke only Arabic, and bowed severely as he spoke to me. But his qualifications showed that he had several years of experience with water training and well rehabilitation—and I've always had a thing for underdogs.

"So you know water work?" I asked the man.

Amir peered up at me with his dark bloodshot eyes. "Yes, yes, yes."

I was pretty sure that was one of the only English words the man knew. But there was something about Amir that I just liked.

"Mr. Dimo, please come back and talk to me this afternoon, okay?"

"Yes, sir," he said with a smile.

"And bring this dude with you too," I said, pointing to Amir.

"Of course, sir," said Hilary, looking a little surprised. "Yes, thank you, thank you."

Amir just nodded reverently and smiled.

As the two men shuffled away together down the dirt street, I couldn't help but notice what an odd pair they made: one tall, educated, proud Christian man and a short Muslim man who forever had his head bowed.

I turned and yanked the Hiring sign off my front door.

FIVE

The UN OCHA compound was about four blocks down the dirt road from my place. Those first few months in Darfur, I attended every single UN meeting I could manage. I'm pretty sure I wore a rut in that dusty path walking back and forth between my compound and the UN's. Actually there was another set of well-worn ruts, those of my friend Andy Shaver, a fellow Samaritan's Purse aid newbie who landed in Darfur about the same time I did.

While I never felt like I fit in well with most of the aid workers I met in Darfur, Andy and I hit it off famously from the start. I knew we would as soon as I caught sight of him rolling into our compound that first day carrying a guitar. He was twenty-six (just a year older than me), a tall, lanky dude with an unruly mop of copper-red hair. He hailed from Vancouver and was well-spoken and obviously well educated. There was a sophisticated urban coolness about Andy.

But he had a down-home side too. Actually it wasn't long before Andy revealed that he actually grew up in Greensboro, North Carolina, not far from where I went to high school. After a while we realized we had some friends in common, and may have even made out with a few of the same girls during high school. Andy had lost his Southern accent over the years, so whenever we told people that we came from the same town, no one ever believed us.

Andy and I kept each other entertained—and sane—as we navigated the international aid world. He was focused on building schools, while I was fixated on water projects. Our favorite UN meetings were the ones when aid workers from all of the different agencies came together several times a week to share information about recent "insecurities" (like reports of firefights, ambushes, or kidnappings).

The meetings were always held at the UN compound, which was slightly larger than ours but surrounded by the same tall walls with broken glass and barbed wire rimming the top. After we walked through the front gate, our first stop was a small concrete room near the front door with a sign-in sheet. A quick scan of the document always revealed the attendance of representatives from a who's who of international organizations—UNICEF, Save the Children, CARE, International Medical Corps, Norwegian Church Aid, Médecins Sans Frontières, and others. There were lots of Europeans, including French, Germans, and Brits, and unfortunately a few of them looked at Americans with disgust. This, upon further investigation, appeared to be born, at least in part, from their hatred of President George W. Bush. Sure, it's a gross generalization, but they felt that Americans were predominantly closed-minded folks, uninterested in the matters of the world beyond the U.S. border.

Though I didn't fit that mold, my cause certainly wasn't helped by the fact that I wore cowboy boots and spoke in a thick Southern accent. Still, it didn't take long for a little Southern charm to break down the barriers.

The meeting room was outfitted with a twenty-foot-long wooden table and dozens of white, purple, blue, and green plastic chairs. Covering the walls were a dry-erase board, a large writing tablet, and lots of maps. There were maps of Sudan and Darfur, city maps, a topographical map, and one detailing regions where current fighting was going on. The seats were always filled during those meetings, and as the worldwide aid response in Darfur grew, the meetings steadily became so crowded that people lined the walls and stood outside straining to listen.

The man they all came to listen to was David Del Conte, the South Darfur team leader for UN OCHA. David was an American, from the Pacific Northwest, and always spoke in perfect, accentless English so everyone in the meeting could understand him well. He was six feet tall with short dark hair, dark brown eyes, and a perfectly trimmed beard, and always wore a freshly ironed button-down shirt with khakis. He was a handsome man who looked like he'd just walked out of the pages of *GQ* magazine. And somehow he always maintained that put-together look, even amid the dust and discord of Darfur.

I'd never actually spoken during one of those UN meetings, but having just hired Hilary and Amir I guess I finally felt like I had something to say. When David asked for announcements of upcoming convoys and such, I raised my hand.

"Just a heads-up, y'all," I said as I stood. "Me and my guys are takin' a convoy tomorrow to check out some stuff up in Kass. Y'all are welcome to join us if you'd like. We'll be shooting up there around eight in the morning."

When I finished speaking, everyone in the room sat there silent, staring at me with blank faces. Even David was confused.

"Can anyone translate what this guy just said?"

Everyone giggled; then Andy raised his hand.

"I think he said something about a convoy in the morning," said Andy.

"Yeah, yeah," I chimed in, a little embarrassed. This time I forced myself to speak more slowly and clearly: "We're leaving with a convoy to Kass at eight in the morning tomorrow, in case anyone wants to join us."

"Oh! Okay," David said with a big grin. "So, anyone who wants to join . . . Wait, what's your name?"

"Doc."

"Anyone who wants to join in on Doc's convoy, just see him after the meeting."

Later that same meeting a soldier with the AU stood up to brief us on the most recent security incidents and alerts for the week. He looked like a big blond-headed rugby player from South Africa, thick and tough as nails. With his heavy Afrikaans accent and a ballpoint pen, he pointed out volatile areas on the map. I also noticed a few other regions outlined in yellow and emblazoned with the words *no-go*. I raised my hand.

"Yes, sir?" he replied, pointing to me.

"So what's the deal with the yellow no-go areas?" I asked.

"Those places are controlled by the rebels and are deemed high-risk areas because of frequent insecurities. They are considered UN no-go zones; no UN personnel are permitted to work there."

"But there are villages and IDP camps located inside those circles? And no one from the UN can get in there to bring them aid?"

"Correct," he said.

"But we can work there, right?"

"Yes, you may go and work in those areas, but only at your own risk."

As soon as he said that, I could feel my heart begin to thump faster.

"If you do choose to go there, make sure you keep in constant communication with us. Tell us when you are leaving, where you are going, and any insecurities you encounter. That way we can support you in the best way possible from here."

After the meeting, I immediately walked up to the map for a closer look. There were two very large yellow-rimmed zones, one in a mountainous region to the north called Jebel Marra, the other southeast of Nyala. Inside that circle were lots of individual villages and IDP camps. The largest camp I could find was called Marla.

That's it, I said to myself. *That's where I'm gonna start my water work.*

While Marla was no more than thirty miles from our compound in Nyala, the drive out there took nearly an hour and a half. For a short way the dusty path parallels the railroad tracks from Khartoum; then it splinters into a spiderweb of interconnected paths that weave in and out of tiny villages along the way. There's no real road, but as long as we kept the truck pointed southeast we were bound to run into Marla eventually.

On our first convoy out there, Andy and I drove in one of our white Samaritan's Purse Land Cruisers, while Hilary,

Amir, and the other nationals with Andy's crew rode in the other truck. We led the convoy but still had fun ripping through the desert, straying off the path wherever we wanted, jumping small dunes and basically just driving like a pair of North Carolina rednecks loose in the desert.

When we finally pulled into Marla I felt like we were rolling straight onto the set of an old Hollywood western. There was a single dusty main street with a handful of shanty shacks, a blacksmith, a mechanic shop, and a couple rickety stands where old women served tea and bowls of oily fried beans called *fool*. No matter where you were in town—day or night—you could always hear the deep guttural *dut-dut-dut* of a single-cylinder engine endlessly grinding sorghum, a cereal grain used as food in this region. Just off the main street sat Marla's largest building, a square concrete structure topped with a flag made of what looked like an old white bedsheet with the letters SLA hand-painted in blue.

Continuing along the main road about a half mile out of town, our Buffalo crawled up a huge sand dune. Cresting the hill, we were afforded a sweeping view of a huge sandy bowl covered in thousands of ragtag tents made of sun-yellowed clear plastic sheets and desert scrub brush. I had seen photos of slums around the world, but this place was terrible.

This was Marla Camp—home to up to ten thousand people, mostly women and children, refugees in their own country.

As we drove into the camp the sandy path narrowed. When we could drive no farther we parked and continued on foot.

Women peeked their heads out of the tents at us while a trail of curious children grew as we walked. I had Hilary ask where we could find the elders of the camp, and an old woman in a sun-faded orange-and-green flowing dress called a tob pointed the way.

The community meeting tent was a three-walled structure made of thick woven reeds. There were six elders wearing light-colored jellabiyas and sitting cross-legged on thin mats inside. As we arrived a tall man in his mid- to late thirties stood to greet us. He had dark eyes, a sharp-chiseled jawline, and an air about him that commanded respect. His name was Ali, a high-ranking rebel leader with the SLA, a respected spiritual adviser from the town of Marla, and the appointed leader of the IDPs in Marla Camp.

Removing our shoes, we joined Ali and the other men on the mats. We knew that with elders like these, serious business could never happen until tea or coffee was shared. As usual, I chose coffee, the traditional Darfuri coffee, black and thick enough to hold a spoon upright. I respectfully asked for *Jebena buna sukar shwaya*; that's coffee with a little bit of sugar. Ali nodded at me with a slight smile and soon our conversations began.

Ali expressed his deep gratitude for our presence. "We knew you would be coming," he said with a smile.

Though he said he had expected us, I could tell he was still quite surprised to see us in his camp. Ali told us we were the first aid workers to arrive there since it was established nearly a year before, with only meager support coming from the townspeople of Marla.

When I asked about their sanitation and hydration issues, Ali explained that the nearest water source for the inhabitants of Marla was a two-hour round-trip walk. Every morning and late afternoon, mostly the children would carry their families' yellow jerricans down a dusty path to fill up.

"It would not be so bad to take that long," he said. "But the water is making some of our people very sick. Some are even dying from it."

"I can help fix that," I said. "I can help your people get clean water."

Ali was obviously very pleased with this.

"Come, come, let me show you our camp. Let me show you our people," said Ali, as he slipped on a pair of mirrored aviator-style sunglasses, then grabbed me by the hand and led me out of the tent.

He continued to hold my hand as we walked. I had heard that Muslim men often show platonic affection with other men by hand-holding, but this was my first experience with it. Ali's hand was rough and strong, and I was completely uncomfortable. Aside from holding my dad's hand as a child, I'd never before held a man's hand, and I wasn't looking to start. Plus, it was late afternoon in the desert, so I was hot as hell—my hand was sweating profusely. But I knew it would have been a huge insult for me to pull away from Ali's grasp. Andy knew this too, but it didn't stop him from shooting me goofy looks as Ali and I strolled through the camp—hand in hand.

After about ten minutes we reached the top of a steep dune overlooking Marla Camp. The sun was diving for the horizon, painting the sand dunes a rosy peach color and illuminating the plastic sheeting. From this perspective, high above this sea of human suffering, Marla Camp actually looked kind of beautiful.

"I want you to know we are very thankful for you and your men coming to help us," said Ali.

"You're welcome, Ali. We'll definitely do our best."

On the walk back to our vehicles, Andy sidled up alongside me, still chuckling. "So how was it, Doc?" he whispered. "Did he slip in the sexy interlocking fingers? Or was it just a regular old handhold?"

"Shut up, Andy."

One of the elders showed us to a small, crudely built brick structure near the camp's perimeter and told us we could use it as our compound for as long as we were there working in Marla Camp. Hilary and Amir gathered dried thornbushes and arranged them into a rough fence around our compound, with enough space to park our vehicles.

Later, while our men slept inside the brick house, Andy and I laid out our sleeping bags in the sand and leaned back to drink in the warm evening sky. Before that night, I thought Montana had the brightest stars in the world, but here there were absolutely no lights to compete with the starry sky. It was blanketed in millions of pinpricks of bright light, so many stars that it made it almost impossible to pick out constellations.

"Man, is there anything else in this world you'd rather be doing right now?"

"Not a thing," Andy replied, staring up at the sky.

"I mean, we're out here in the field, meeting Ali and all these cool folks, and I'm getting ready to bring them clean water, and you're building schools for their children. Did you see the smiles on those elders?"

"Yeah. This is what it's all about, Doc," he said. "We're finally getting a chance to do the kind of work we came all this way to do."

"I'm so fired up, man. I just can't wait to get out there and get it done."

The next morning I went to work figuring out ways to get clean water to the inhabitants of Marla Camp as quickly as possible. The best option seemed like drilling a well right there in camp. But paying another organization to bring their drill rig all the way out here proved to be both expensive and nearly impossible, since this was a UN no-go zone. However, through a contact from those UN meetings, I eventually arranged a temporary solution—a huge fifteen-by-ten-foot, 2,500-gallon water bladder from UNICEF. I erected a pair of tap stands right there in the middle of Marla Camp and then paid for a local driver named Abdulla to start trucking in clean water to fill the bladder.

From: Doc Hendley
To: Joel Kaiser, Samaritan's Purse
Sent: Monday, October 18, 2004, 2:57:19 p.m.
Subject: Here's some numbers

OK, I'm taking the truck down in the morning. The truck holds 7,560 L of water. It comes with a pump, a driver, and fuel. The total cost for 4 weeks, 28 days, is . . . 1,120,000 SD; this is $4,307.69 if the exchange rate is 260 to 1. I am working on a budget but I will be able to better guess quantities after tomorrow's trip. And, yes, I will try and get some pictures for you tomorrow. I am bringing down the tanker full of water so I can fill up the bladder first thing in the morning.

Have a good one bro,
Doc

It was a simple, low-tech solution—but it worked. As the pillow-shaped bladder began filling and the first jerricans were topped off, the inhabitants of Marla Camp erupted into a joyous chant of *"Moya! Moya! Moya!"* And I watched with a deep smile as the children started running around like crazy—it was the first time I'd ever seen them play in that camp.

Visions of the faces of those women and children, with their first jugs of fresh water in God knows how long, fueled my desire to do more. Trucking in water (four times a day) wasn't sustainable long-term, and we were still having trouble finding a rig to bring in to drill a new well.

"Look, Mr. Doc, there are probably some other wells around here that just aren't working," said Hilary hopefully. "Maybe we could just fix them."

Ali answered, "Yes, yes, there is one by the school, but it has dried up. It hasn't worked for five years."

"Will you take us there?" I asked.

Right there in Marla, in the front yard of the local school, was a galvanized-steel hand pump encircled with a low ring of cement and a small fence to keep livestock away from the water source. The concrete was cracked, the fence broken, and the pump was overgrown with weeds.

"Are there many other wells like this around?" I asked Ali.

"Oh, yes, indeed," Ali said, grabbing a map and a pen. He drew small Xs in spots where other wells could be found. There turned out to be dozens within a ten-mile radius of Marla, many of which were only broken.

With that information, my men and I drove back to Nyala in the hopes of sourcing the appropriate tools for well repair and some spare parts. Both Hilary and Amir had some experience repairing wells, and through my UNICEF contact we got what we needed. In no time we were back at the well in the schoolyard.

Slowly, methodically, Amir, Hilary, and I began disassembling the well. First we unbolted the hand pump and then began pulling out the well's guts. The pump was connected to a long rod that manipulated a valve deep inside the well to pump water up the pipe. (It's a pretty simple design that works in much the same way as a human heart valve.) We used long pipe wrenches to muscle up the narrow steel pipes that reached the groundwater some hundred and fifty feet below the surface. Each section of pipe was nine feet long, and as soon as each was raised aboveground we had to secure it with a clamp before lifting the next. Eventually we got to the end of the line and raised the pump itself from the hole.

"It's still soaking wet! It's fricking wet!" I yelled.

"At least the well hasn't dried up, Mr. Doc," agreed Hilary.

"Yep, there's still water down there. We can make this work. I know we can."

Carefully we laid the pump on the sandy ground and began dismantling it piece by piece. I pried off and replaced a few rubber seals that had disintegrated, while Amir and Hilary worked to replace several corroded lengths of pipe.

There was definitely plenty of trial and error, but four hours later we had the pump totally reassembled and began the painstaking process of lowering it back down into the well.

As I tightened the final bolts on the hand pump I noticed a bunch of young children leaning out the front door of the school, watching us intently.

I gave Amir the nod and he slowly started pumping.

Nothing happened. He kept pumping. Still nothing. I could see sweat pouring off his thick brow.

Then suddenly there was a gurgling sound. It grew louder, and soon water began spurting out of the pump. With that, the children came running out to the well. They smiled and pointed and I could hear shy whispers of, *"Moya, moya."*

Sure, it took us most of the day to fix this well, but I was shocked at how easy it actually was to get it back up and running. In all it cost us a total of only about thirty dollars in parts, versus the approximately six thousand dollars it would have cost us to drill a new well.

That became our team's mission: finding and fixing broken wells. For the next several weeks we drove all over Marla and the surrounding villages, locating derelict wells and bringing them back to life.

From: Doc Hendley
To: Jeff Hendley
Sent: Saturday, October 9, 2004, 3:51:13 p.m.
Subject: Howdy

Howdy,

Well, it hasn't been long since my last e-mail but I felt like I should inform y'all on what's going on this weekend.

The team is going on an assessment in a rebel-controlled area called Marla. This area is southeast of Nyala and is right in the middle of the conflict. Our team has felt called to help in Marla, and the surrounding area, mainly because other organizations refuse to work in the rebel controlled areas. This means that the IDPs (internally displaced persons) in that area are desperately in need of aid. Samaritan's Purse has had a good relationship with the rebel armies of Sudan in the past and we think we can continue that here in Darfur.

The number one cause of death, by far, in the world today is waterborne diseases. We have already been on one assessment to Marla and have found that almost every well is in non-working order due to faulty pumps, broken pipes, and loss of pressure. This causes the people to try and find water on their own. If the people are able to find water it is usually contaminated which, as you know, is not a good thing. We are anxious to get to Marla to help give the people food, shelter, and medical supplies, but the most important thing for these people is clean water. Remember . . . an average person can live over a month without food, but if they are without water they will die after 3 days.

Many of you have asked how you can help or how you can get involved. Well . . . first and most important . . . pray. . . . If some of you feel like you want to give to the project, my father and I have set up a way for it to go directly to the project in need. *Please* don't take this as a "call for offering" or some crap like that.

Anyway . . . we have already had a lady designate $3,000 for clean water, and I intend to match that with some of the money that we raised with Wine to Water back in the spring. Wine to Water is the fund raising organization that I started with help from my dad and one of my friends, Tasha, at the beginning of this year.

That $6,000 can go to help drill one well in the area that we are surveying, or it will go to fix the broken pumps on the existing wells. If you want to help support the water project you can send some dough to my pops and he will wire it straight into our Samaritan's Purse projects account.

I'm sure my dad will write another e-mail on where to send the money and how to make out checks. We do have 501(c)(3) status, and everyone that wants it will get a receipt for tax purposes. At the moment we will work on as many projects in the area that we have funding for. So, if you have a few thousand burning a hole in your pocket, don't use it for something cool like buying a motorcycle, give it to a village in Africa. . . . :)

It is also quite possible that Tasha may throw another Wine to Water bash or two, so that we can raise money for more wells, water bladders, and pumps. If she does you should go, because it will be a blast . . . and have some extra fun for me since I can't be there.

Someone else has donated their time to make us a website in the next few weeks as well, so that should be up and running soon. I will try and post pictures and info on the site, whenever it does get going, that way everyone can keep up with what is going on in the water project and y'all can have some pictures to go along with it. Thank y'all so much for your love and prayers. Peace out!

W/ Much Love,
Doc

Over the next three weeks we made seven trips back and forth from Nyala to the Marla region, fixing six wells and bringing fresh water to three thousand more people beyond Marla. Meanwhile Andy had been busy establishing school programs for the children of Marla Camp. He built a thatched schoolhouse, similar to the one used by the elders for meetings, and established an incentive program to attract teachers to come and teach at the camp.

Besides his being a good friend and coworker, I felt like Andy's education work melded well with the water work I was doing. On the most basic level, I was helping the children get access to clean water so they could be healthy and grow, and Andy was helping those same children to develop their minds. In my opinion, those are the two most important needs in any community—education and clean water.

As we continued getting things accomplished, Ali was obviously increasingly pleased with our progress. One evening he even stopped by our compound to invite Andy and me to dinner at his home.

Ali's house lay on the outskirts of the town on the road to Marla Camp. It was a typical Darfuri hut, with a thornbush fence and a decent-size yard with a couple dogs and a few goats and chickens. Ali's wife was a few years younger than he and had given him two children. She had a sweet smile, but we would not be able to get to know her, as she was busy cooking and serving us, and in this conservative Muslim culture men and women rarely share meals together.

Andy and I played with Ali's young children as he sat back and drank his tea. Witnessing his kids and his warm home life helped me see Ali more as a loving family man, rather than just some gnarly SLA leader.

After a hearty meal of fried goat and fool, he offered us some seeco, a homemade liquor similar to the moonshine made in the North Carolina mountains, except instead of corn it was made from crushed dates. There were plenty of reasons I should've turned it down: 1) Samaritan's Purse strictly forbids drinking while in the field; and 2) according to Sudanese law, those caught drinking alcohol would get a steep fine and lashing. But I'm a bartender, and I hadn't had a drink in over sixty days—the longest dry stint I'd endured since I was probably about eighteen. So I decided to drink the seeco. It was a clear liquid with a bitter aftertaste, and it burned my throat the same way moonshine does. I loved it. And it must've meant something to Ali that we shared a drink with him, because later that night he invited us to be his guests at a secret meeting of the SLA rebels.

We followed Ali through the moonlit streets to a place in the dunes not far from Marla Camp.

"Can you frickin' believe this, Doc?" whispered Andy. "We're going to a secret SLA rally."

"I know, man; this is huge!"

When we arrived, there were nearly ten thousand people already seated in the sand—it was a sea of people. Before sitting down, Ali introduced us to Mohamed Isa, one of the SLA's top commanders. He wore the dark khaki uniform of an officer. It was well pressed and fit tightly, since Isa was pretty chunky. With Darfuris, you could always tell who was wealthy and important by how much body fat they carried. Although he wasn't armed, he didn't really need to be, because Isa was flanked by a hulk of a guy who was the toughest-looking AK-47-toting soldier we'd ever seen.

Isa thanked me and Andy for helping his people and told us to give him a call if we ever ventured to the mountains of Jebel Marra. With that, I whipped out my little notebook and jotted down his Thuraya satellite phone number.

Then Ali led us to a spot right there in the front row of the massive crowd. As soon as we sat, a man in an SLA uniform of dark green camouflage grabbed a megaphone, stood in the bed of a truck, and started yelling to the crowd.

Neither Andy nor I had a clue what he was saying, but it was obvious that this was some kind of SLA pep rally. The speaker would shout something; then the crowd would cheer or chant, "SLA! SLA!" in response.

I can't speak for Andy, but I was actually starting to get into it when suddenly an elderly woman in the crowd stood up and started yelling something at the speaker. Again, I didn't know what she was saying, but it was obvious she was upset. And it was obvious that the speaker didn't like what she was saying. Almost instantly a handful of SLA soldiers armed with AK-47s appeared from the shadows and started pushing their way through the crowd toward the angry woman, who was now working to blend into the anonymity of the crowd. The speaker kept yelling something, probably asking for the crowd to give her up. Eventually there were fingers pointing, and a pair of SLA soldiers swooped in and grabbed the old woman. She yelled and screamed wildly as they dragged her through the sand—and then there was no more screaming.

I leaned over to Andy and slowly whispered out of the side of my mouth, "Holy shit."

Before that moment I had been convinced that these SLA guys were fighting for a noble cause and doing so in a noble manner. But now I wasn't sure of anything at all. While I was confident Andy and I were safe and would continue to be so as long as we kept building relationships with these guys, I wasn't convinced the SLA's motives were simply to protect their people. I mean, why were they seemingly forcing their own people to follow their agenda? I had no idea what we had just witnessed, but I did realize that going forward I should be more savvy. This crisis was far more complex than simply the good guys versus the bad guys. And I would probably be best served by focusing on my water work rather than trying to figure out all the politics swirling around Darfur.

SIX

In the Muslim religion, Friday is the holy day, with obligatory public worship held at noon. Naturally very little work could be accomplished on that day, so Friday became our de facto day off. Truth is, we were in such a groove of working that we probably never would have taken a day off if it wasn't for the holy day.

Most Fridays, Andy and I would just hang out at our compound, writing e-mails to folks back home, reading, listening to music, and doing whatever else we could come up with to pass the time. Sometimes I couldn't wait till dark so I could go to sleep and just get on to Saturday, when we could get back to work again for another six days.

My bed was wooden-framed with tightly strung nylon roping instead of a box spring. On top of that lay a three-inch-thick yellow foam mat. At the time I thought it was the most comfortable bed I had ever slept in, but looking back it was probably just because I was terminally exhausted, either from working long hours in the heavy African sun or fighting off the latest worm or parasite I'd picked up from the local food or water.

At night I kept a small electric fan pointed directly at my face to keep the flies and mosquitoes away. There was some risk of malaria in Darfur, so I was issued a mosquito net. But it was woven so tightly that it severely reduced airflow, and I found it too hot to sleep inside of the net. Actually I was also supposed to be taking preventive malaria medicine daily, but I gave that up too after a few weeks.

From: Doc Hendley
To: Tasha Craft
Sent: Friday, October 29, 2004, 4:24:44 a.m.
Subject: Yo, darlin'

GREAT PHOTO! I laughed the longest I have since I've been in this godforsaken country. I won't be here this weekend. I am rarely at the compound anymore. I have been out in the field for about 4 or 5 days out of each week. It would be best to talk when I go on r&r. I ain't

really sure when that is, though. my 60-day mark is this
Wed. but it will be later than that, I think. So, you'll just
have to take lots of Halloween pics and send them to me
with a full detailed story of the evening's events. Man . . .
I had a dream two nights ago that I went home and I
bought this old school phat ass chopper and I was riding
all over creation with it. it was by far the best dream
I've had since I've been here, especially since last night
I dreamed about a plane crash. oh well, have a good
Halloween. I wish I could be there. When I come home
we will have a Halloween part 2. We can all get dressed
up and raise hell.

Well, I'll talk to you later darlin',
doc

One afternoon in late October, Andy and I were in the Nyala
market shopping for some goat meat and fresh vegetables
when we spotted something across the aisle near a pile of
mats and ornate rugs.

"Holy crap, Doc, look at that thing!"

"Hell, yeah, Andy," I said. "We gotta have that for the
compound."

It was a monster TV satellite dish, probably eight feet
across, and made from hundreds of flattened silver vegetable-
oil cans with the letters USA printed in dark blue. These cans

were likely provided to the IDPs by a U.S. aid organization, and, like most everything else in this country, once they were emptied the locals found inventive ways to reuse them.

We hadn't watched TV in months, so we quickly bargained with the shopkeeper for the dish and an old-school twenty-six-inch color TV, complete with a receiver box. Even though we didn't know if it would actually work or not, the immediate flood of excitement we got from the simple notion that we might be watching TV soon was worth the risk.

Andy and I raced back to our compound like a couple kids on Christmas morning, anxiously awaiting the shopkeeper's delivery of our stuff. Before long we heard him clanking down our street, the dish and TV covering his rickety wooden donkey cart.

Hilary was handy with electronics, so we had him climb onto the roof and mount the dish. Then I held my breath as Andy hooked up the last of the wires to our TV. There was lots of fuzz. Then, suddenly, a picture snapped onto the screen.

Soon we found what appeared to be a music channel, the Middle Eastern equivalent of MTV. From then on, Andy and I spent many a Friday hypnotized for hours at a time by the strange music and dancing of Middle Eastern pop stars. The songs weren't exactly my style, and we didn't have a clue what they were singing about, but I loved it. In fact, I'd be lying if I didn't admit that I soon developed a schoolboy crush on a sultry brunette Lebanese star named Nancy Ajram. I credit her in part for the motivation to work on my Arabic.

The only thing that could snap us out of our music video–induced daze was a blackout. Actually the power went out daily, and blackouts often lasted for many hours at a time.

That was when we would whip out our guitars.

Andy and I sang and played together a lot. He sounded a bit like James Taylor, and loved that sort of Americana-style storytelling music. I gravitated toward classic country music. Together we sounded like some pitchy cocktail of Johnny Cash, James Taylor, and the Counting Crows, or maybe a couple of dying dogs—but it didn't matter to us. We loved playing together and thought we sounded pretty dang great, especially those times when our songs were fueled by a night of seeco drinking.

We had heard news that Samaritan's Purse was sending a new fellow to Nyala to work with us. All we knew was that he was pretty young and from Boone, North Carolina, not far from where my parents were living. Finally, one Friday morning in late October while Andy and I were just sitting there staring at each other, he arrived.

His name was Jonathan Drake, and when he hopped out of the Land Cruiser onto that dusty Nyala street he looked just as silly and green as I had looked two months earlier when I first arrived in Darfur. He was dressed head to toe in khaki safari-style clothing, with his shirt tucked in and his pants pulled up high. Jonathan was twenty years old, with dark brown short but unruly hair. He outweighed Andy and me by at least forty pounds—which wasn't such a feat, considering we were only tipping the scales at around a hundred and fifty pounds each at that time.

Jonathan's nasally voice was a dead ringer for Ned Flanders, a character from *The Simpsons* cartoon, and I can't say I was surprised to hear that he'd been homeschooled. Jonathan seemed like a garden-variety oddball, but when he pulled out a small guitar case I changed my tune. All I could think about was that Fridays might not be so boring if we could put together a three-piece band.

Saturday brought more work, and as always I was excited to get back into the field, where I could accomplish something. Things were really coming along with our water projects in Marla. In addition to installing the bladder in the middle of camp, we fixed two wells in Marla, as well as eight others in the surrounding villages, like Sania Afandu and Hijar. And there was lots more to do, so I hired a few extra nationals to join my team.

I hung up my Hiring sign once again, but the men I eventually hired came recommended by Hilary and Amir. My first new hire was named Simon Drailey, a thirty-year-old Christian from the Dinka tribe in the South. Just like Hilary, Simon was university educated and spoke excellent English (aside from a stuttering problem that popped up whenever he was scared or nervous). He became one of my main translators. He was also very computer literate and provided critical assistance writing up reports and the many grant applications necessary to get supplies for our water projects from UNICEF.

Ismael was my next new hire. Much like Amir, he was a quiet workhorse and a devout Muslim. But Ismael stood prouder and taller than Amir because he came from a slightly higher social class. His English was about as bad as Amir's, though he brought some valuable well- and pump-rehabilitation experience to our team.

Finally there was Hamid, who was like a combo of the best parts of Ismael and Simon. He was a hardworking Muslim in his early thirties with some field experience in water projects, but he'd also studied some in the local university, so his English skills were pretty good too.

Without planning it, I had assembled a perfectly balanced team of three Muslims and three Christians (including myself). Sure, everyone prayed differently and at different times of the day, but we were all bonded by the common goal of bringing clean water to the IDPs of Darfur.

The more UN security meetings I attended, the more I heard the name Jebel Marra, and it was almost always mentioned in relation to some unstable security situation: rebel clashes, kidnappings, etc. Obviously the place was also considered a massive UN no-go zone.

Jebel Marra is a volcanic mountain range located in central Darfur about eighty miles northwest of Nyala. In Arabic, the name means *bad mountains*, but it's actually a zone of temperate climate and high rainfall with fertile volcanic soil—an oasis amid this endless desert.

The mountains were inhabited by the Fur ethnic tribe and had long ago been forgotten by the Sudanese government in Khartoum, which had provided zero infrastructure there. There were no roads, no electricity, no telephones, no hospitals. And the Fur people's feelings of being forgotten by their own country were part of what fueled their uprising against the government. The mountains became the SLA stronghold, closely guarded by the rebel armies and seemingly just out of reach of the Janjaweed and government fighters.

But that didn't stop the Janjaweed. Since they couldn't take the mountains, the Janjaweed instead systematically destroyed the surrounding villages that provided supplies and logistical support for the mountain villages. Besides killing countless innocent villagers, they also regularly attacked the roads in and out, strangling many of the valuable supply lines to Jebel Marra and driving thousands of people fleeing into the hills to makeshift IDP camps, which were then essentially unreachable by international aid organizations.

Knowing there were so many people in Jebel Marra in need of help made me ache to go up there. So I put together a plan. Hilary would take over as team leader, continuing to rehabilitate wells in the Marla area with Hamid and Ismael. Simon, Amir, and I would head for the mountains.

In order to reach Jebel Marra, we first drove fifty miles

or so north of Nyala on one of the only paved roads in all of South Darfur. Once we got to a pair of side-by-side villages named Mershing and Menawashi, we steered east directly toward the very center of the Darfur region and drove another thirty miles or so on a dirt path. Actually, calling it a path is being generous.

Along the way to the base of the mountains we passed through an area historically trafficked by nomadic Arabs, and thus the Janjaweed, as they grazed their livestock north to south. Nearby was the town of Melem, a base for the Janjaweed fighters. Obviously its proximity to the SLA stronghold was a big reason this area was so notoriously dangerous to travel.

My senses remained on high alert as we bumped along that path. I was shocked by what I saw, or rather, what I didn't see. There wasn't a single soul on that entire stretch. We passed through small farming villages but they were all empty. Some were burned to the ground, completely destroyed by the Janjaweed. Others, like the village of Teige, were simply deserted, eerily absent of human life, like some mighty force had come down and swooped away all its inhabitants, leaving the village like a still life in a time warp. Many of those villagers likely fled south to form new IDP camps near Nyala; some may even have been living in Marla Camp.

As we pulled into a small town called Kidingeer, the gateway to Jebel Marra, I slowed the Land Cruiser, looking for signs of life. Suddenly a teenage boy leaped into the road from behind a baobab tree. He was dressed in a filthy camouflage uniform with an AK-47 that was half as tall as he was. He pointed the gun in the air. We pulled closer and he fired a warning shot. We stopped the truck near what looked like an old school and he quickly began walking over to meet us. Soon more young soldiers appeared, seemingly out of nowhere, and gathered around our truck.

These boys were all SLA soldiers, and when I was their age I was running around in the woods of North Carolina hunting squirrels with my BB gun. I couldn't help but think they should probably still be sitting at the desks inside that school instead of pointing automatic rifles at us. Through Ali and the SLA outpost back in Marla, we had obtained the sat phone numbers of several key rebel commanders in Jebel Marra. And we had left a message with Mohamed Isa. They were expecting us, and as soon as the boy soldiers realized who we were, they greeted my team warmly.

Before moving on up the mountains, the boys led us to the backside of the school to a spot where the Janjaweed had executed all of their teachers and some of their schoolmates. The mud-colored brick wall was splattered with bloodstains and bullet holes, and judging from where the bullets had pierced the wall it was clear where the teachers had been executed and where their shorter students had also once stood.

It was a gruesome sight. My stomach turned. And then it was as if time slowed down. The colors of the world around me, the trees, the schoolyard, the boys' uniforms, it all faded into black and gray.

How in the hell could someone yank little boys and girls out of their classroom, line them up along the school wall, and shoot bullets through their skulls? I screamed to myself inside my head. *Who could do that?*

Never before in my life had I tasted hatred like that day, standing in the abandoned schoolyard. It welled up inside my gut. It burned inside me. I wanted nothing more than to beat the living crap out of those evil Janjaweed soldiers.

I was still in a haze as we drove away from Kidingeer.

"You okay, Mr. Doc?" asked Simon.

"Yeah. Yeah, I'm fine."

I tried to push those emotions back down into my gut. As we made our way up the steep hills, the anger and disgust welled up higher.

Our trucks continued climbing, winding up the eastern slope of Jebel Marra. I concentrated on driving, and was continually impressed by the Land Cruisers' ability to scale these volcanic rocks that would have been difficult to walk, much less drive up. As we slowly made our way, thick vegetation began growing all around us. The colors finally made their way back into my vision, bringing me again from black and grays to rich Technicolor.

The landscape was breathtaking. It was the most green I'd seen in the past two months since I'd landed in Darfur, and it sent my brain swirling with memories of a time seven years earlier, when I used to call the mountains of Montana my "home."

I was eighteen, partying hard, and had just dropped out of college after completing my first semester. I guess I wasn't ready yet. The way I looked at it, I had just been through twelve straight years of school, so why in the hell would I want to jump right back into four more years? I knew there was a big world out there waiting to be explored beyond those classroom walls, and I wanted to taste it.

About that time I got a phone call from my aunt and uncle out in Montana saying one of their friends was looking for a ranch hand. He needed someone to help work the young colts, preparing them to become either high-end cutting horses or team roping horses. That was all I needed to hear. I promptly packed all of my possessions into the back of my old black Ford pickup, loaded my Harley onto a small wooden trailer, and I was Montana bound.

For ten months, I lived on the River Bend Ranch on the outskirts of the small town of Bigfork in northwestern Montana. It was nestled in the Flathead Valley along the cottonwood-covered banks of the Swan River. Nearby stood the towering granite peaks of the Bob Marshall Wilderness, and in the distance, to the north, lay Glacier National Park and, beyond, the mighty Canadian Rockies.

I grew up a lot on that ranch. I learned the meaning of truly hard work, stepping up when there was more to be done, even when I thought I was too exhausted to continue.

Uncle John taught me a lot about being a man too. He was rough around the edges and drank beer and smoked, but he was also a dedicated Christian—he even led a Friday-morning Bible study for ranchers, construction workers, and other hardworking guys in the area. But Uncle John wasn't anything like the annoying, rule-toting Christians whom I knew back home. He taught me that I didn't have to be perfect or have all my shit figured out to believe in God and be a Christian.

Bottom line, I really respected Uncle John, I loved Montana and, after about ten months, I left that ranch a better man.

With Montana holding such a special place in my heart, with Jebel Marra looking so similar, and with the horrors of the dusty desert now seemingly far below, it was no surprise that I was quickly falling in love with these mountains.

As the day wore on, the path became tighter and steeper, almost impassable in places, until we finally arrived at the small village of Feina. I hopped out of the truck and deeply inhaled the cool, dry mountain air.

A crowd of curious, smiling villagers swarmed around. Obviously word must've spread up the hills after our stop in Kidingeer. These folks had rarely before seen outside aid workers in their village.

About that time the crowd seemed to part, and an older man walked purposefully toward me. He had a weathered face, a scruffy gray beard, and a flowing traditional jellabiya.

Although he looked eighty years old, he was probably only about sixty. As he approached, the man reached out in welcome, grasping both of my hands.

"*A salam alaikum,*" I said, greeting him with my sloppy Arabic.

"*Wa leicu salam,*" the man responded warmly—roughly translated: *And peace be with you.*

"*El humdelilah,*" I followed. His smile brightened as I attempted to speak his language.

"*Nam nam, el humdelilah!*" he said with a smile: *Yes, yes, praise be to Allah.*

Meanwhile Simon was falling over himself as he hurried around the hood of the Land Cruiser to translate. He didn't want me to think he wasn't doing his job, but I liked speaking Arabic and enjoyed trying to stammer through this small talk.

The old man gripped my right hand tightly, which I was getting used to by this point, and led me down a narrow path toward a small, empty round hut beside a larger, square mud-and-rock building. He gestured for us to sit down with him on a mat that was already laid out. Almost immediately two young women appeared with tea and coffee.

With a cup of hot tea in his palm, the old man began speaking again. This time, Simon was ready to translate.

"I am the sultan of this region," he said. "And I praise Allah that you have come here to help our people. We have been waiting for someone to help us from our suffering, but we thought that the Janjaweed would frighten everyone away. But you have come anyway to help our people. Praise Allah."

The sultan went on to describe the terrible Janjaweed attacks in the villages nearby and how the Janjaweed now controlled the road that we had arrived on. For several years, those fighters had hijacked nearly every supply truck headed for the sultan's villages. I had never before met a true sultan, and I hung on his every word.

"Not many trucks make it here anymore," he said solemnly. "We have to try and live off what we can grow and what livestock we have left."

I listened, spellbound by the horrors as he went on. There wasn't much I could say or offer.

Several cups of coffee later, the sultan said, "We welcome you here and want this to be your home while you are here. Take this place where we are now as your own to stay and work from, and . . ."

Simon abruptly stopped translating.

"And what, Simon? What did he say?" I demanded.

Simon's eyes got really big and he smiled wide, showing his bright white teeth.

"What?"

"And, h-h-he s-s-says," he stuttered, "'I wo-would be most honored if you wo-wo-would ma-marry my daughters.'"

"What?" I exclaimed as honorably as I could. "Marry his daughters?"

Simon strained to swallow his laughter. I did the same, trying not to offend the very generous sultan.

"He s-says they are v-very beautiful, Mr. Doc."

"Does he want me to have more than one of his daughters?"

"Yes, there are two left and he wants you to have them both."

"Tell the kind sultan that I am honored by his offering me his daughters, but tell him that I am already promised to someone back in the U.S."

This was a lie, of course, but it was the nicest way I could figure to turn him down. The sultan looked a little disappointed, but his smile soon returned as we continued sharing coffee and tea. Meanwhile Amir was busy building a fire in the hut next door and setting up a place for me to sleep for the night.

Later I dug into a care package that my mom had sent me via Jonathan Drake. It was full of handwritten letters from my family and friends, plus a handful of cigars. As I lay there on my sleeping bag puffing away and reading one of her letters, I paused and thought to myself, *I love what I'm doing. For the first time in my life, I feel like I'm actually doing something that's larger than myself.*

When I woke the next morning, the sultan was right there waiting to drink tea with me again. We never ate breakfast first thing in the morning, because the Darfuri locals could afford only two meals each day. Generally they would take tea early in the morning, then work until around ten or eleven, when it was finally time for *fatoor*, or breakfast. The next meal, *asha*, or dinner, was always saved until after the sun went down.

Over my morning coffee, I had Simon translate, telling the sultan we needed to explore the area so we could see what problems they had and what we could do to help. I made it clear that I was focused on bringing them clean water, which the sultan assured me was their most desperate need. But I also told him about Andy and how he could help establish schools in the region, while some of my other colleagues might even be able to bring in food. I promised to bring them back with me to Jebel Marra on a return trip.

The sultan was amazed. I could tell he was on the verge of tears, but then he quickly stood and walked away. I turned to Simon.

"What's that all about? Is he okay?"

"I'm not sure, Mr. Doc."

He soon returned to the hut, leading a mangy dark brown horse.

"If you want to see the other villages in this area and see how much we are all suffering, you are going to need this." Simon translated the sultan's words. "Your truck cannot take you where you need to go."

The sultan offered me the horse's reins. I bowed my head slightly.

"*Shukuran geezera*, Sultan," I said, thanking him.

He gave me some directions to specific villages in the hills, which I inputted into my handheld GPS so I could find my way back to Feina. I said good-bye to Amir and Simon, and I was off, galloping away into my newfound Montana.

From: Doc Hendley
To: Jeff Hendley
Sent: Sunday, November 17, 2004, 3:26:07 p.m.
Subject: What up?

Howdy,

I guess it's been awhile since I wrote. I have been out in the field for most of the last week or more. As I said last time, our team has a heart for the rebel controlled SLA areas so I have been in those places establishing relationships with the rebel soldiers and the commanders. I didn't realize just how important those relationships were going to be until I found out that 20 people from NCA (Norwegian Church Aid) were captured and taken to Marla where they stayed prisoner for 5 days by the same rebels that I was working with. So, while I was there hanging out and eating with these SLA guys they had 20 people held captive somewhere in the same village. But I still feel very comfortable with the rebels; they actually remind me a little of the southern people back home. They are very down to earth and family-oriented. Even these big time rebel commanders love to chase the children around and make them laugh by making goofy faces and noises. They became rebels because they weren't getting enough representation in gov't and they are mostly made up of an agricultural type society, whereas the bigwigs in Khartoum are all about money, oil, industry, etc. Not to mention the tens of thousands of people that the Janjaweed and gov't have killed.

Anyway, I have found the Montana of Sudan. Those who don't know, I lived in Montana for a short while and I still have close family in northwestern Montana. Since my first visit there over 10 years ago I have felt like it was my home and that I would one day raise a family there. So, anyway, my "Montana" in Sudan is called Jebel Marra. It is a mountainous volcanic region in Darfur and is one of the most beautiful places I have ever seen. The weather is great and the people are fantastic. However, there is an eeriness about it. When we reached the first village, called Kidingeer, we found it deserted except for the boy soldiers half our age that surrounded us with AK-47s. They were rebels, so they were legit, but it is humbling to know that when I was these boys' age I was shooting BB guns and learning how to open my locker in middle school.

In this ghost village there is a place you can see where the Janjaweed lined up people against the schoolhouse and shot them. There are bloodstains and a bullet holes behind where the people's heads were.

After leaving Kidingeer we passed through many other burnt-out villages till we reached the higher elevations and made our way to the small village of Feina. There are still a large number of killings in the areas surrounding Feina, so most of the people go up and sleep in caves at night. But, there were a few who felt comfortable to stay in the town with us because of SLA presence. I met the Sultan of the region who was head of about 100,000 people in the surrounding Jebel Marra area. He was way cool. The next morning after we all feasted—oh yeah it's Ramadan so they don't eat or drink in the day and at night they feast—this Sultan came to me and asked me what else I needed to do. I told him I needed to assess the rest of the area but it was tough because the people were so spread out and our vehicles couldn't drive in the mountains. So, he gave me his horse and I took off into the mountains alone and met with the people that lived up in the hills surrounding Feina. My Arabic was still meager but I had learned enough of the language to get around and gather the basic information I needed about their water situation. It was an awesome sight to behold on the one hand, but at the same time, it made me hurt, as I met numerous people whose family had been killed by the Janjaweed.

While traveling I met a young girl named Howa. She is five years old, and is the cutest little African mountain girl. But, last month Howa was shot along with some other women and men in her area. The local "doctor" put salt and a makeshift cast on her arm where the bullet went through and broke the bone. When I saw her, she was sweating from a fever and her arm and hand below the bullet wound were swollen to double the size of her other tiny hand and arm. Please pray for Howa. I sent her and her family to a real doctor from Nyala. I haven't heard if she was seen, but I hope and pray that the doctor was able to help her.

Like I said, Jebel Marra is absolutely gorgeous and the people appear to be downhome-type mountain folks, but these things are merely on the surface. Underneath there is a plague of evil haunting and forcing them to hide in caves when the sun recedes behind the towering mountains. I know I sound like a broken record, but please pray for them. They want to live in peace and sleep in their own little mountain huts without dragging their children off to a cave every night to hide from the Janjaweed.

Well, I wish I could write down everything, but if I did I'm sure I would have already written one more novel than any of you wants to read. Thank you again for your prayers and support. I am proud to have such great friends and family. I am so sorry that I can't write more e-mails, but my r&r is coming up soon so I hope to catch up with everyone in the next few weeks. I love you all . . .

Doc

P.S. The water projects are moving right along. We already have a water bladder in place in the rebel area of Marla, and we will have a water tanker stationed there this week along with a team that will fix broken pumps. I'll try and have some photos by the time I go on r&r.

As we drove back to our compound in Nyala from the mountains, my head was awash with the possibilities up in Jebel Marra. In addition to the broken wells, I found out that there had been many cholera outbreaks in the region, a vicious waterborne disease that can wipe out half a village in a matter of days. Luckily, with chlorine tablets and a little education, it's actually pretty easy to prevent.

During my assessment, I was also informed that the Jan-jaweed destroyed one of the major dams in the area over a year earlier. It had been one of the main sources for drinking water and much-needed irrigation. With that, I started thinking about what I could do to help rebuild the dam. I didn't know the first thing about cholera or fixing dams, but I figured it was just like back when I first started bartending in Raleigh: It's not so much about how good and fast you are at making a Fuzzy Navel; it's about developing a good relationship with the people sitting in front of you at the bar. Get that down first and then you can learn how to mix the complicated drinks—or fix a dam.

After I got back from Jebel Marra, I was pretty sure the heels of my cowboy boots must have grown somehow, because I was walking taller than ever.

How much better could things get? I thought to myself. It didn't take too long for us to bring water to thousands in Marla, and now the people of Jebel Marra would be next.

I was fired up to get started.

A couple of mornings later, back at our compound in Nyala, I was sitting on our leopard-print foam couch and sipping my morning coffee when Andy came running in. He had a pale look of dread on his face.

"Dude, I just got off the phone with Jonathan."

"Yeah? What's up?"

"He was on his way back into Marla when he ran up on the Sudanese military. They were waving him back and trying to get him to turn around when the whole frickin' place erupted in gunfire. Jonathan whipped the truck around, and as he was speeding off he saw a helicopter gunship flying toward Marla."

"Shit! Amir's in Marla now," I blurted out. "I sent him down there yesterday."

"Oh, man, that's not good," Andy said, pausing. "I think Marla is gone."

SEVEN

From: Libbi Hendley
To: Doc Hendley
Sent: Saturday, December 11, 2004, 1:57:00 a.m.
Subject: More questions

Doc,

I was just reading some news and found something
interesting. Are you near Mistiria, Jebel Marra mountains,
Tawila or Thabit? All of those places were mentioned in
some of the articles that I just read. The article also spoke
of around 10,000 IDPs that have disappeared from the

Marla area. Isn't that where you are? Or near where you
are? It also said that some NGO staff had to be relocated.
Are they wanting to relocate your team too? Oh well as
you can see I'm full of questions and I'm not sure if you
can answer any of them or not. But I had to ask.

I love you and hope to hear from you soon,
Mom

As soon as news of the attack made it to the UN and the AU
authorities, they immediately launched a helicopter assessment mission. In fact, they arrived in time to witness the
Janjaweed fighters still looting the camp and setting everything afire. I tried like mad to get in touch with someone,
anyone, who could help me find out if Amir had survived
the attack on Marla Camp. But I turned up nothing.

The next morning, a second team, including my friend and
next-door neighbor David Del Conte, and an AU rep named
Brian Steidle, was scheduled to do another assessment and sift
through the destruction. David asked us if Samaritan's Purse
would like to send someone along, since we were the only
NGO working in the camp, so Andy joined them. Before he
left I pleaded with Andy to keep an eye out for any sign of
Amir. I felt responsible for putting him in such a dangerous
situation. If he was dead, I wasn't sure I could forgive myself.

The team returned later that evening. But there was no

sign of Amir. All they found was a gruesome scene. David invited me and Andy next door to his compound for drinks.

"It's not good, man," David said to me, after taking a long sip of Scotch.

"And obviously it's not looking so good for Amir, either," added Andy.

"There were dead people everywhere," David said, staring blankly into his glass of Scotch as he described the destruction. It was evident that the Janjaweed, probably working in concert with the Sudanese military, had systematically killed as many of the people in the camp as possible, before stealing all of their livestock and possessions and burning the entire place.

Next to a large baobab tree they found the body of a middle-aged woman who appeared to have been huddling over a bunch of young children during the attack. She was using her own body to shield as many kids as she could, but there was nothing more she could've done. Some kind of ordnance had exploded nearby. Her body was torn apart, and there were body parts of children hanging in the broad branches of the tree.

"Some of our guys were out scouting the surrounding desert," he went on. "They found quite a few children not far from Marla, facedown in the sand, dead from dehydration. They were too afraid to go back to Marla and couldn't find any water and just couldn't make it any farther."

The same anger I'd felt at the schoolhouse in Kidingeer started to rise again from my belly. Images of what the attack must've been like flashed through my brain. Then they shared some of the photos from the assessment. It was even worse than what I had been visualizing in my mind.

"The good news is, your water bladder is still intact," explained Andy.

"Well, that's something. I really gotta get more water trucked in there for the people who are still hiding out in the desert," I said, now with a glimmer of hope. "They'll probably come back looking for the water."

"Good luck getting your truck in there," said Andy. "The Sudanese military has already set up an outpost just outside the camp."

"I'm going back," I said.

"Be careful, Doc," warned David. "I'm pretty sure there's Janjaweed all over the place."

"I don't care. I'll make friends with whoever I have to so I can keep water in that bladder."

"What are you gonna do, just drive in there and say, 'Take me to your leader'?" Andy said with a chuckle.

"Yeah, that's exactly what I'm going to do."

I found the soldiers on the side of the road leading into Marla, right where David and Andy had told me they'd be. As Hilary and I pulled up in our Land Cruiser, a pair of young soldiers in fatigues shuffled up, guns leveled at our windshield. They could have been Janjaweed or with the Sudanese military; it was tough to tell.

I rolled down the window and spoke the simple Arabic greetings I knew, and then Hilary began translating.

The water bladder in Marla Camp, just after
being filled up for the first time.

This picture of a young boy from Marla and me was taken during
the camp's first food distribution. The camp can be partially
seen in the background. *(Photo by Tim Holmes)*

I took this picture on one of my initial visits to Marla Camp.
It is a classic African scene of women and children
beginning their long journey for water.

Giving a mini concert from the hood of the Buffalo with my
travel guitar for the people of Sania Afandu.

My team fixing a broken well. Ismael is in the yellow shirt,
and Amir is just below him in gray.

Guys from our team fixing a well not far outside Marla in a village
named Hijar. The well had been in non-working order for five years
before this day. Hamid is on the left, and Amir is on the right.

These young girls were watching our team
as we fixed the first well in Melem.

Two young boys walking toward Sania Afandu from Marla.
This picture shows the typical topography of Darfur.

Coy and me before a night of boxing. Coy is on the right with the short hair, and I am on the left with the unkempt hair and beard. *(Photo by Andy Shaver)*

Me in the middle of a boxing match with Coy.
(Photo by Andy Shaver)

Me and a group of rebels.

A Land Cruiser full of antigovernment rebels checking in on us near Marla.

Boy soldier Mustafa.

Mustafa taking the last few puffs of another soldier's cigarette.

One of our trucks rolled off the road in Jebel Marra while taking a
load of blankets to villagers living high up in the mountains.

Giving a water filter to a family in Haiti just after the 2010 earthquake.
(Photo by Lisa Ballantine)

"They are saying, 'Why you here? What are you doing here?'"

"Tell them I don't want to talk with them. I only want to speak with their commander—that's it," I said.

With that, the pair of soldiers began shouting. Hilary shouted back. He too was getting mad. The argument continued to grow to a fever pitch.

"What are you saying to them, Hilary?" I shouted.

He didn't respond. He just kept on shouting at the soldiers in Arabic.

"Hilary! Do not say to them anything but what I tell you! You understand? Do not say anything on your own," I shouted. "You are my voice, my translator; you do not speak on your own!"

"Okay, Mr. Doc."

"Just tell him we want to speak with their commander," I said. "That's it."

"Okay, okay," said Hilary, and began translating my words to the soldiers. "He said he will take us to the commander but only if he can ride with us."

Hilary scooted over on the bench seat toward me as the large soldier squeezed into the front seat with the barrel of his AK-47 sticking out the passenger-side window. He pointed the way, leading us through Marla's now empty streets lined with charred buildings and on toward the IDP camp. There was a handful of military tents pitched on the outskirts of Marla Camp. Ironically, they had built their outpost right beside the schoolyard where I'd fixed that first well.

As soon as they saw our truck, more soldiers piled out of the tents and stormed toward us. But once they realized one of their own was in the front seat, the soldiers lowered their weapons.

The soldier riding with us hopped out and quickly returned with a man who was obviously their commander. He wore dark khaki and carried a Thuraya satellite phone on his belt.

"This is the commander," Hilary translated.

"This time, please, only speak what I say," I pleaded to Hilary. "That's all. Please do not respond to his questions, because they are directed to me, not you.

"I have a gift for you," I said, gesturing toward the commander. As Hilary translated, I produced a carton of Benson & Hedges cigarettes that I had bought for him earlier that morning. The commander smiled.

"Look, I don't know what went on here, and it's not my business to know," I said.

"We didn't do this," said the commander. "We don't know who did."

"It's not my business to know. What I do know, though, is that there are many children and women out here hiding in the desert. And I do water work. That's my bladder in there. Please just allow the man who drives the water truck access into the camp so he can keep filling it up, just in case there are people around who might be coming back for water."

The commander studied the carton of cigarettes as Hilary translated my words. He opened it and fished out a box and eventually a single cigarette. The commander rolled it in his fingers, smelled it, then looked back my way and began speaking.

"He says yes. Tell the driver he can start bringing water today. It's no problem."

"Thank you, sir. Thank you."

We all shook hands. I was pumped as we drove away from the outpost. And I couldn't wait to get back to Nyala so I could tell Andy that my crazy plan had actually worked. On the way back to our compound I called my driver, Abdulla, and told him he could resume trucking in the water immediately.

Later that afternoon, word came that Amir was alive. He was indeed working in Marla Camp when the helicopter gunship began firing its rockets into the camp, but he ran like hell. Fifteen miles later he arrived in the little town of Sania Afandu, where just a week earlier we had fixed a well. We immediately sent a truck to fetch him while Andy and I celebrated with a swig of seeco.

With Amir safe, and water now being trucked back into Marla Camp (I'd even heard that some IDPs were starting to filter back into the camp), I was now able to concentrate on my plans for Jebel Marra. I worked with my contact from UNICEF to address the cholera outbreaks up there. He helped me arrange for short-term bucket chlorination of the drinking water there, and I wrote up a grant to get chlorine tablets, which we'd then distribute to as much of the population as possible. Longer-term I needed to figure out how to get a drill rig up the mountain to establish some new wells near the villages.

I remembered that on the first visit, the sultan had told me that supply trucks often had trouble making it to his villages over the past year, so they were in desperate need of NFIs, especially blankets. The mountains did get really cold at night, so I arranged for a monster truckload of dark gray wool blankets to accompany me on my next assessment in Jebel Marra. Getting my trucks up the mountain seemed easy this time. The sultan was very appreciative of getting the blankets, and I told him that next time I returned I'd bring supplies to help his people with their water issues.

A few days later, back in Nyala, I was in my room working on some grant applications when there was a knock at our compound door.

"Hello, Mr. Doc," said a young man in his late teens, his eyes looking very urgent. "I am Abdulla's son, the driver of Marla water truck. He's been hurt and he wants to see you."

"What happened to him?" I asked. "Is he okay?"

"I take you there."

We hopped in my truck and Abdullahh's son led the way as we sped through the narrow dirt streets of Nyala. We ended up in the southwestern portion of Nyala in a "middle-class" part of town. I quickly followed him through the front door of a basic concrete home and immediately saw his father lying on a mat on the living room floor. His face was bloody, with deep purple bruises already forming. Both of his eyes were swollen, the left one nearly swollen shut. He had literally been beaten to a bloody pulp.

"Holy crap, Abdulla."

"Hello, Mr. Doc," he mumbled. I could tell it hurt for him to move his lips.

"Don't get up, Abdulla. What happened?"

"This morning, I went to fill up the bladder in camp. It was my second trip. But when I get there I was attack by Janjaweed. They shoot my truck, shoot holes in my water tank. Then they pull me out of the truck and beat me. They shot holes in the bladder too. I'm sorry, Mr. Doc; Marla is finished. They attacked whoever was left there. It's finished."

"Oh, man, Abdulla," I said, sick to my stomach. "I'm the one who should be sorry. I met with the soldiers. They promised me they would keep you safe and let you fill the bladder. I'm so sorry this happened."

Abdulla grunted a thank-you and tried to smile while his family stood at his side with worry on their faces.

"You just stay here and get yourself better," I said, touching his shoulder gently while handing his son a wad of cash to pay for his wages, plus a little extra to help with doctor bills and such. I felt like shit as I walked back out that door.

What's going on? I thought to myself. *First I almost get Amir killed, and now I get my driver beaten to within inches of his life.*

I felt responsible for all of this. There I was, trying to do something good. Trying to make a difference in people's lives. And then this happened. Marla Camp was a total loss. Was there something more I could do to help there? Maybe I should just shift my energy to helping the villagers up in Jebel Marra and keep my pump-rehab teams roaming around villages a safe distance from Marla.

About a week later I headed back to the mountains. Our trucks were packed with tools, wheelbarrows, and such to help the villagers maintain the roads so we could one day possibly get a drill rig up there. The motivation was also partly selfish, as on our last trip up, one of our trucks actually rolled right off the poorly graded road.

Once again I was driving the lead truck, with Simon riding shotgun. After Hilary's lackluster translating work, I decided to use Simon. Hilary stayed behind in Nyala to do hand-pump work with Ismael and other team members. The rest of my team, Amir and Hamid, followed me in the Buffalo.

It was midday; the heavy sun was lording it overhead. Not a cloud in the sky. And hot. It was my third trip up to Jebel Marra, and I was getting used to seeing all of the burned-out villages along the way. Actually, becoming numb was more like it. But the school near Kidingeer with its bul-let holes and bloodstains still always messed with my brain. This time I would be prepared for it, though.

As we drew closer I could see a small column of smoke rising above the low rolling hills from a spot just east of the school. A pit began growing in my stomach. The vegetation here, mostly mukheit bushes, much like desert sage, and tall, dried grass, grew thick. The road took a sharp bend to the right. And just then I could see men on the side of the road dressed in jellabiyas burning bushes, grass, and brush. *What in the hell are they doing?* I thought. As I watched, confused, they set more fires, and a group of five or six armed men in camouflage jumped into the road in front of us. One of them raised an AK-47 and fired a warning shot into the air. I slammed on my brakes to avoid hitting them. The Buffalo was tailing me so tightly that it had to swerve around us as it skidded to a halt.

"What the hell are these fricking SLA guys doing?" I said to Simon, irritated. "I called the sultan two days ago. His boys know we're coming."

I leaned out the window and waved the soldiers over. "Yo! *Salama! Asma!* Listen, come here!" I yelled out the window. The soldiers walked closer, mean eyes focused on mine.

"As soon as I tell them what we're doing it'll be cool," I said.

"Simon, ask them what the hell is up," I said as I rolled down my window. A clean-cut, older-looking soldier leaned over to peer in our window. *"A salam alaikum. De shinu!?"*

Simon was shaking his head back and forth while stuttering, "D-D-D-D-Doc! N-n-n-n-n-no. N-n-n-n-not S-S-S-S—"

"What, Simon?"

More soldiers were surrounding our trucks, guns trained on us.

"What are you guys doing? I already spoke with the sultan. I'm bringing his villages supplies," I shouted at the men.

Simon was shaking. "N-n-n-n-not S-S-S-S-L-A. J-J-J-J-J-J-anjaw-w-w-w-e-e-d."

By the time he finally got the words out of his mouth,

my stomach sank. I watched as a pair of soldiers opened the doors of the Buffalo and yanked my men out of the cab. Other soldiers jammed their guns into my men's heads. They forced Amir and Hamid onto their knees with their hands behind their heads.

"Oh, shit!" I said as a soldier cracked Hamid's temple with the butt of his AK-47 and he toppled over into the sand. The impact of the gun to his head sounded like a watermelon hitting the pavement.

By now the Janjaweed commander was staring at me through my half-open window. I slowly began rolling the window back up.

"Tell them to stop!" I shouted at Simon. "Tell them to stop!"

"La-la-l-l-l-l-la," he stuttered, as another soldier began yanking on his door handle, trying to get Simon out of the truck. The commander was motioning for me to open my door. But I refused. And I left the truck running in case they started shooting and I needed to gun it out of there. The commander yelled forcefully at me.

"What's he saying, Simon?" I demanded. "You need to settle down. I need you to speak to me, tell me what he's saying."

"F-f-f-f-f-f-f-f-f-f-f-f . . ."

At this point Amir and Hamid were now facedown in the sand.

The soldiers rifled through the Buffalo, tossing shit on the ground and taking all of their stuff: watches, shoes, shirts, and all the tools in the bed of the truck. In the rearview mirror I spotted a pair grabbing our gear out of the bed of my truck.

The soldier jammed the barrel of his AK-47 into the back of Hamid's head.

"No, no, no, no!" Hamid pleaded for his life.

"Simon, I need you to take a deep breath and tell me what this dude is trying to say."

"Wh-wh-wh-wh-wh . . ."

It was no use. His stuttering was out of control. I watched as another soldier pushed Amir's face into the dirt.

"Malesh, malesh," I yelled to the commander. "I'm sorry, I'm sorry. I'm working with *moya*, water. I'm trying to help the people. Just water."

The soldier cocked his AK-47 and screamed at Hamid as he rammed the barrel into his head again.

"H-h-h-he's s-s-s-saying he's g-g-g-going to kill him," said Simon, finally speaking more clearly. "H-h-h-h-he's going to sh-sh-sh-oot him."

"Malesh, malesh!" I shouted again.

Suddenly the commander looked toward the soldier with the gun trained to Hamid's head. He yelled something at the other soldier. They started to argue. Eventually the soldier raised his weapon with disgust. The commander looked at me and said something in a very stern voice.

"Simon, what is he saying?"

"H-h-h-he says he's going to let us g-g-g-g-go. Going to let us g-g-g-o. H-h-he's not going to kill us. But if they ever see us w-w-w-w-working in this area, they will k-k-k-k-k-ill us next time."

He waved his arm at us, shooing us away like a swarm of flies. Something seemed to just click in his head. We probably should've died that day. But for some reason the commander let us go. Maybe he was connected with the government of Sudan, and killing aid workers would've blown his deal. Or, hell, maybe it was divine intervention.

Amir and the rest of the team climbed slowly back into the Buffalo, and together we turned our trucks around. The soldiers kept all of our gear, but at least we were leaving with our lives.

As we drove around that big turn, I kept an eye on the rearview mirror. Suddenly all the soldiers were gone. All I could see was the thick green mukheit bushes and a slender column of white smoke rising above the hill. Just like that, gone. It was almost as if the soldiers were never there. But they remained vivid in my mind—an unwelcome memory that tattooed itself on my brain.

Simon and I didn't talk much as we drove back toward Nyala through the bright afternoon sun.

EIGHT

From: Doc Hendley
To: Tasha Craft
Sent: Saturday, December 18, 2004, 1:57:00 a.m.
Subject: Coming home

I think I'm pretty definitely possibly coming back on
the 17th of Jan., SO we gotta get movin'. I want to have
a wtw bash that Thursday that makes the other one
look like naptime in pre-school (I loved naptime though).
anyway, we gotta BLOW IT UP. I got some ideas I need
to chat with you about sometime too. Maybe me, you,
and my pops can talk about it in Jan. I'm thinking of

trying to raise enough money with wtw to buy our own drilling rig. I've been getting trained in drilling. It kicks ass yo. Well, I'll try to call you later, or you can try to get me. don't let the beans spill too much. I hope to have my ticket reserved on Monday though.

later gator,
Doc

After every ninety days or so of work in the field, Samaritan's Purse allowed us to take a ten-day R & R—that's rest and relaxation. My first R & R fit its name well. I flew to Mombasa, Kenya, on the Indian Ocean coast, and I did nothing except sit on the beach drinking beer the entire time. I probably didn't speak more than three words (*beer*, *please*, and *thanks*) that whole week, but it was exactly what my brain needed to decompress.

For my second R & R I headed all the way back home to North Carolina to see family, and for another Wine to Water event. Just getting out of Darfur was always a total mission in itself. First, I had to fly Midair Collision to Khartoum, but then I had to board plane after plane on a thirty-hour marathon back to Charlotte. It was the first time I'd returned to America in six months, and I wasn't prepared for the shock.

The first shock I had was walking off the plane and into the frigid January air. My body had finally become acclimatized to the oppressive dry heat of the desert. Actually, whenever the nighttime temps back in Darfur dipped into the eighties, I thought it was freezing. That was compounded by the fact that I'd dropped about twenty pounds, weight that my already lean frame didn't need to lose in the first place.

Naturally I was excited to see my family again, but I was surprised by how nervous I was. As I shuffled down the stairs with my blue backpack slung over my shoulder, I spotted my mom, dad, and brother Bo waiting for me. Mom's eyes lit up as soon as she saw me, and then she started to cry. I hugged everyone, but it felt like I was just going through the motions. My arms were hugging, but I didn't feel anything. I was numb. I was staring a hole through a brick wall in baggage claims.

"Doc, you smell like crap, son," said Dad. "I'd hate to have been the poor sod who had to sit beside you on that flight. You're really skinny too."

I did smell. And I'd lost so much weight that my features were slightly sunken in. My face had an almost angular look. I had to laugh, because I was starting to look sort of like the Darfuri I'd been working so hard to help.

"You look good, honey," said Mom, holding my hand tightly as we walked. "A little bit skinny, but you look good."

As we pulled out of Charlotte Douglas International Airport and straight into six lanes of afternoon traffic, I was shocked by how fast everyone was driving. Cars and trucks were flying past all around us. The speed made me nervous. But at the same time, everything seemed so orderly. Everyone was driving in nice straight lines, staying in their lanes, one behind another. There was no honking or people leaning out the windows to shout at one another. Back in Darfur I rarely drove over twenty mph, and although the roads of downtown Nyala were always packed, it was a slow kind of chaos. Donkey carts and tuk tuks, people and livestock walking every which way—yet I had come to understand it. It was finally making sense, and I appreciated the Darfuri pace of life.

The three-hour drive from Charlotte to Raleigh was pretty much one big blur. The rolling hills and forests of the piedmont, the faded red tobacco barns, the bright winter sun. It was all just one endless colorful blur.

The conversation was a blur too. My family was asking me all of these questions. I had to tune it out, the same way I tuned out my teachers back in high school. While I under-stood logically why they were so interested in Darfur, I had no idea how to respond. How could I begin to explain what I'd experienced those past six months? The way the desert always seemed to crack in pieces under my feet. The pungent smell of burned fool in the afternoon. How Hilary always laughed at my jokes, or the sound of the butt of that gun cracking Hamid's head. Meeting a five-year-old girl who had a hole ripped through her shoulder by a Janjaweed bullet. And the way seeco reminded me of moonshine. And how I felt every time we found water sloshing at the bottom of a broken well. Where would I even start?

So I mostly responded with two- and three-word answers.

I could tell my dad and brother were confused and getting irritated. But Mom, she seemed to understand.

"Look, guys, I'm sorry if I'm being distant. I guess I just don't really know what to say right now. . . ."

"It's fine, Doc. We're just glad you're home and that you're safe," she said. "Don't feel like you need to talk, but know we're here if you need to."

Back in Raleigh, my dad had organized a celebration dinner at a local steak house for our family and some of my best friends. We all got dressed up—I was wearing a gray buttondown shirt and black slacks—and I felt totally uncomfortable in those clothes.

I watched as the waiter poured everyone at the table tall glasses of ice water. Then I opened the menu.

Holy shit.

The prices averaged about thirty dollars per plate, and I was floored. Back in Nyala, I'd become accustomed to paying twenty-five cents for a full meal. And thirty bucks? That would pay Amir's or Hilary's wages for two weeks.

My stomach churned as I looked at the tables around me. All those plates of beautiful food. I used to love eating out—that was why Dad picked this place. But in the past six months, food had become something of a nuisance to me, a hassle. Eating had become a chore that I had to do a couple times a day only because my body needed the calories to keep going—so I could keep working. In Darfur, the only time food is celebrated is during the month of Ramadan, when people fast during the day and feast at night. Other than that my standard fare had become fool or canned tuna, with a shot of vinegar and hot sauce.

The Wine to Water event was held at a college bar in Raleigh, not far from the Hibernian Pub and my old stomping grounds. It was another success—we raised nearly five thousand dollars—and everyone was there, my entire Glenwood Avenue bar crew. It was like a homecoming in a way.

Now, I can't tell you how many nights I'd sat alone in the desert sipping on crap seeco, playing out that very night in my mind over and over. I'd be right back there in Raleigh, sitting at the bar, and everything would be the same. The event would go well, we'd raise a bunch of money, and then my crew and I would rage late into the night for old times' sake.

It didn't go exactly like that.

I tried sitting at the bar, drinking whiskey with all my old friends and talking about last night's hockey game, who was sleeping with whom, and all the same crap we used to talk about. But it wasn't working. It felt awkward. And surreal.

One after another someone would inevitably ask me something about Darfur. Yet I realized I had no more than sixty seconds before I'd lose them. Their eyes would glaze over. These are good folks, and they cared about me and what I was doing over there. But I guess at the end of the day, they were simply too far removed from the world that had become my life to understand. I'd just flown from a world where children and their parents were literally dying all over the place, where there wasn't enough food to eat or water to drink, and my friends couldn't, or didn't want to, comprehend it.

And I can't say I blame them at all. When I was in Raleigh, I was living a totally carefree lifestyle. I didn't worry about much at all past Glenwood Avenue and my little crew of friends. Sure, I started caring about Wine to Water and trying to help bring water to people, but until I actually landed in Darfur and started really seeing the problems and caring about those people firsthand, none of it was real.

In all fairness, it was I who had changed. In fact, I probably changed more, mentally, emotionally, and spiritually, in those last six months than I had in my entire life. I was a different person walking off that airplane in Charlotte. And, in a way, I had to relearn how to relate to my family and friends again.

My good friends Tasha and Ubie were the only ones who were different. I guess they had invested so much more into me as an individual, and Tasha had spent countless hours helping the Wine to Water effort while I was away. Neither of them really understood my rambling stories, but they listened.

That night really defined a lot about who my true friends were.

It was very depressing in a way too. I didn't feel like I fit in with my old bar crowd anymore. And Darfur is tough as shit, and I didn't really fit in with the career aid workers there. I mean, I was just some redneck bartender trying to make some kind of difference. So where was my place now?

I never could've imagined I'd be happy to leave Raleigh,

but I was relieved to get back into the car again. We were headed south to Greenville, South Carolina, for a get-together with my entire extended family. While I wasn't looking forward to another barrage of questions from my family, I couldn't wait to see my granddaddy Dick again.

His real name is Dickson—just like me—but everybody just calls him Dick. He grew up in the 1930s in the slums of Greenville. His family had no money, but thanks to his skills on the baseball and football fields, Dick was able to get by—and eventually get out of the ghetto. He was such a well-loved football star in high school that businesses along his walk to and from school would feed him breakfast and dinner each day. Dick eventually landed a scholarship at Clemson University playing football and baseball. He was an all-American in both sports and went on to play professionally as a running back with the Pittsburgh Steelers.

Back then it was nearly impossible to make a living as a professional football player, so after two seasons he quit and started his own janitorial service. He humbly cleaned toilets, mopped floors, and mowed lawns. Over time Dick grew that business into a multimillion-dollar company that now handles maintenance contracts for textile mills, hospitals, warehouses, and such.

It's the classic rags-to-riches tale. Today, Dick and my grandma Lucille live in a twelve-thousand-square-foot mansion in a country club in Greenville. And I have the utmost respect for Dick, because he earned every bit of what he has.

Dick remains a pillar in my family, a soft-spoken, self-made man who deserves attention whenever he speaks. To me, he is my hero. Dick is John Wayne himself. He's always been a hard-looking man, with a big square face and strong jaw. He's big boned, six feet tall with a full shock of gray hair. If he were a dog he'd be a boxer or a mastiff.

I loved sitting with Dick in his den as he chewed tobacco and told me stories of football and fighting and chasing girls. My parents named me after Dick, and I wanted to grow up to be just like him.

When we arrived at Dick and Lucille's home, there were already thirty people there—aunts, uncles, cousins, everyone. They'd all signed an oversize welcome-home card covered in lots of pictures of me in Darfur that they'd printed from my e-mails.

Lucille cooked a huge spaghetti dinner, just like she'd done countless times for these big family get-togethers we'd been having all my life. Usually Dick was the focus of these dinners, but this time everyone wanted to talk with me. Asking me questions. Trying to get me to tell them stories.

But I wasn't used to all this action and attention. Back in Darfur I had tons of downtime. It may sound sort of surprising, but I spent the bulk of my time in the desert just being quiet. I spoke very little Arabic, so even when I was out in the field with my crew I never actually talked that much. So all this attention from my family was overwhelming. The walls were closing in on me. My hands started shaking uncontrollably. I needed to get away. From everyone.

So I flew out of the living room and shut myself in one of Dick's many guest rooms. There, beside the bed, I crumpled to the floor, a sobbing mess, curled up in the fetal position. If there's ever been a point in my life when I've felt like I was totally out of control, this was it. I was absolutely freaking out.

When my parents came in to check on me I was shaking uncontrollably, mumbling, "I gotta get out of here. I gotta leave. I can't be here right now."

My mom gently rubbed my head as if soothing some vulnerable child as she and my dad helped me slowly pull it together.

Then my dad went back out to the living room and told the others that I just needed some space, that I hadn't been myself since I'd gotten back. Though it was all perfectly true, I don't like showing weakness. And I've never been so embarrassed as that evening when I came out of the bedroom and returned to my family.

I retreated again, but this time I went to the den, where Dick was alone, sitting in his recliner, watching a college basketball game. I took a seat in the chair right beside him, grabbed a plug of the tobacco he was chewing, and sat there quietly.

We just sat there for at least an hour. It was nice, the not talking. Then Dick shifted in his big leather chair, turned to me, and said, "Doc, I'm proud of you."

NINE

Not long after I returned from my R & R, we received word from Samaritan's Purse headquarters that they were sending another aid worker our way. But this wasn't just any worker—it was Coy Isaacs, the son of Kenny Isaacs, the fellow who had sent me to Darfur all those months ago.

At first I was very skeptical of Coy. I don't know why. I guess I just pictured him as a "coach's son" kind of guy, who only got the job because of his daddy. Andy and I were both worried that he'd come in all high-and-mighty. A know-it-all. And there's nothing I hate worse than a know-it-all.

But Coy wasn't like that.

I was packing up the truck with supplies for a pump-rehab trip when Coy arrived at our compound. He was in his early twenties, thin, with dirty blond hair, and he actually looked a fair bit like me, just a little bit younger. But as he hopped out of the Land Cruiser, I was surprised to see that he didn't appear totally green, like the rest of us had when we'd first arrived. No safari clothing, no fake black beard, no silly homemade African shirt. Coy wore his regular street clothes and seemed sure of himself. Not cocky. It simply looked as if he'd done this before.

And he had.

Coy was born in North Carolina but was raised in East Africa for several years while his dad did fieldwork, and then he went off to a boarding school in Kenya. At eighteen, about the time I was out working on that ranch in Montana, Coy was in Bosnia. He'd been itching to do something in the big wide world, so his dad sent him off to do aid work for Samaritan's Purse right smack in the middle of the Bosnian war and genocide.

"So, what are you hoping to work on while you're here?" I asked Coy. "Any specific areas of interest?"

"Nah, I'm just ready to get to work," Coy said. "I know sometimes it takes awhile to get plugged in, but I'm up for anything."

"Well, I'd love to have your help running my hand-pump team. They are a bunch of good guys, and right now they're working southeast of here, in Sania Afandu."

"Yeah, sounds good," he said.

"Cool. I'll be back from Melem in a couple days, and then you and me can shoot out with my team."

"Right on. Looking forward to it," he said to me as I hopped into my truck.

Melem is a village northeast of Jebel Marra, about a two-hour drive from Nyala. It's a Janjaweed stronghold and home to the folks who had, eight weeks earlier, hijacked our convoy on the way to Jebel Marra, beaten the ever-loving crap out of my team, and promised to kill us if they ever saw us again.

So why in the heck would I be going to Melem? Good question. It's actually the same question that was posed to me by both Andy and Jonathan.

Here's how I saw it—the Janjaweed had already destroyed Marla Camp, and now they were trying to prevent me from going back to Jebel Marra and the folks whom I felt called to help. So my only hope to continue working there was to go to Melem, fix a few of the wells in the bad guys' hometown, and pray that word of my good deeds would find its way back to them. It'd be kind of like a bribe so that my team could get back to the mountains. And it'd be a way to demonstrate to them (and to myself, I suppose) my belief that every human being in this world, regardless of race, religion, or political affiliation, deserves unconditional access to clean water.

Both of our vehicles were loaded down with tools, piping,

and other repair materials. I wanted to be prepared with everything we might need so that we could arrive and start fixing wells immediately. I wanted to show up and do something right off the bat, rather than doing an assessment and talking about how we planned to help.

I brought my best guys on the trip, Amir and Ismael, with Hilary back on as my translator. After the last translation debacle during our hijacking, I left Simon back in Nyala to do paperwork. I had settled on Hilary as the lesser of two evils. Hamid refused to join us for the trip to Melem, and I couldn't blame him. For some reason the Janjaweed soldiers seemed to specifically have had it in for him, beating him like a dog. I never figured out why, but I knew he'd be better off in Nyala working with Simon. While none of my other men made public their disapproval of my plans to go to Melem, they were indeed quieter on this trip, not as chatty as normal, and definitely on edge.

The closer we got to our destination, and the deeper into Janjaweed-controlled territory we drove, the more nervous I became. With every hill we crested and large tree we passed, anywhere I thought someone could be hiding, I held my breath. At every turn I half expected to see the Janjaweed storming down a dusty hill on horseback, mowing us down with automatic gunfire. I tried to relax and loosen the death grip my fists had on the steering wheel. It was surreal, like I was driving straight into a dream.

As we rolled into Melem, I took a deep breath and did my

best to gather my thoughts. I was ready to go to work. Driving through town, I realized that things looked slightly nicer than every other village we'd worked in so far. It wasn't as put together as, say, Nyala, which was flush with Western aid money, but as far as villages go it was definitely much wealthier. There was lots more livestock roaming around, homes were well kept, and the women's clothing was brighter and cleaner than elsewhere. I soon realized these were the spoils from the Janjaweed's ongoing looting of other villages throughout the region.

Usually when we arrived in villages for the first time the locals smiled, waved, and even cheered as we drove in—ecstatic that aid workers had finally arrived to help. Not here. They simply stared at us like, *What in the heck are you guys doing here?* The villagers weren't hostile at all. It was more as if they were in shock to see us there.

I drove straight through town until we found the market, which I figured would be the best place to find a community leader. The Melem market was set alongside the sandy banks of a dry wadi. Much like the rest of the town, this market was nicer than others we'd seen around Darfur. There were several neat, clean rows of stalls, probably fifty stalls in all, each a wooden skeleton with thatch covering the roof. Only about half a dozen of the stalls were occupied, as it wasn't an official market day, so we approached the first person we encountered—an old woman selling vegetables.

"Hilary, ask her where we can find a local sheikh to talk to," I said.

The old woman simply pointed down the dusty road toward a small tent sitting under a baobab tree.

It was a three-sided structure built with woven reeds. Inside a lady knelt over a little makeshift charcoal stove, roasting coffee beans over the fire and brewing tea. The smell was comforting, like the way my parents' wood fireplace back home in Boone smelled. Several older men sat on low wooden stools drinking tea. And, sure enough, there was our sheikh, a man with a long gray-and-black beard in his mid-sixties wearing a bright white jellabiya. The man looked confused as I greeted him, doing my best with my broken Arabic.

"Hilary, please tell him we've been doing water work in this entire area. We've been going to Jebel Marra and some other villages. Tell him it's our intention to help everyone who has not been reached by aid workers. Make it clear to him that we only do water work and nothing else. And ask him if there are any wells in this area that need fixing."

Hilary translated. The sheikh just looked at me. Then his gaze moved to our trucks, full of pipes and tools and men ready to work. Slowly the sheikh raised his arm and pointed across the market.

"He says at the main school in town the well there hasn't been working for years, so the schoolchildren have to walk long distances to get their water every day, taking them from their studies," translated Hilary.

I nodded and smiled, but what I really wanted to say was, *At least these kids are still in their schools, and your men haven't dragged them out back and shot them in the head like they did to those other kids right down the road.*

Instead, I said, "All right. Ask him if he'll show us the way, Hilary."

Sure enough, right there in the schoolyard sat a derelict well. It was covered in sand, and it was obvious it hadn't been used in quite some time.

We didn't say much; we just pulled out our tools and began working. By that point, my team had fixed probably forty wells across the region, and we had become a well-oiled pump-rehab machine.

Slowly a handful of locals began gathering to watch us work. At first there were just a few schoolchildren; then the adults came too. Before long there were sixty-odd villagers staring at us. You'd think with that many folks watching there would be lots of commotion. But it was quiet. Just a few whispers and low mumbles. They weren't giddy and happy like other villagers in other parts of Darfur. These folks watched us carefully, cautiously, as if they were thinking, *Wait a second, we're the bad guys. Why are they helping us?*

They *were* the bad guys. It was their men who were doing all the raping, the murdering, burning down villages and IDP camps—and I wanted to smash their teeth in. But, I reminded myself, the children in the crowd were still innocent. They didn't know the difference between right and wrong or understand war. They probably didn't even know what was going on beyond their own village.

It was morally difficult for me to fix that well, but I knew we had to do it if we ever wanted to be able to go back to Jebel Marra and help the folks I really wanted to help. Those schoolchildren were the reason I was able to stomach it. And, after all, they still deserved clean water. It's a simple human right.

This is for the children, Doc, I told myself over and over. *We're doing this for the children.*

As we groaned and strained to pull the heavy pipes from the ground, we realized this was the deepest well we'd ever attempted to fix. It was just under two hundred feet deep, much more than the suggested hundred-and-fifty-foot maximum for this type of hand pump.

Sweat poured down my brow and stung my eyes. It was slightly less blistering here than down in Nyala. I guess the higher elevation and the wind might've helped lower the temps slightly, but it wasn't a refreshing wind, more like someone was aiming a huge hair dryer in my face as I worked. Still, it was one of those classic Darfur desert days, with a bright cobalt sky and not a single cloud anywhere.

When we pulled the last of the pipes up, it was wet. Nearly every well we'd worked on in Darfur was still wet, yet we always seemed to be surprised when we found water at the bottom of an old nonfunctioning well.

That one took us about five hours to fix, a couple hours longer than others because it was so deep and needed more replacement parts than usual. But we repaired it. And although there was no chanting of *"Moya! Moya!"* as we began pumping fresh water from the ground, I could see it in those children's eyes: They were excited because they knew they no longer had to trek hours for water.

We found the sheikh back in the coffee tent, just as when we had first met him. He looked pleased when Hilary told him that we had successfully repaired his well at the schoolyard.

"Hilary, please tell the sheikh we're here to help anyone and everyone. The whole politics of this issue and why the fighting is going on—that's not our business. Not our concern. We're here to give water to all the tribes," I said. "And ask him if there are more wells around here that might need fixing."

As Hilary translated, the sheikh frowned a little at first, then began gesturing with his hands, pointing this way and that.

"He says there are quite a few more. Three more right here in town. And more broken wells on the outskirts of the village."

"All right," I said. "Tell the sheikh I'd love to bring my men back and continue working here. We'll go back to Nyala, get more supplies, and in the next couple of weeks you'll see me or my men back here to fix more wells."

With that, the sheikh's demeanor changed. He shook my hand. Even grinned a bit. I was stoked. I was sure that word would soon spread throughout the village, and hopefully on to the Janjaweed soldiers, that the guys in the white trucks with the big blue SPs emblazoned on their hoods came and fixed broken wells in their own village.

As soon as I got back to Nyala I began planning my return to Jebel Marra.

From: Doc Hendley
To: Jeff Hendley
Sent: Saturday, March 19, 2005, 12:04:16 p.m.
Subject: What's happenin', what's happenin'

Thanks everyone for all the e-mails today. Y'all sure do know how to make a boy feel special! I didn't really have much of a birthday other than the e-mails. I went to Melem . . . the village where the hijackers came from. I didn't get shot at or anything, so I guess that is kind of a birthday present. I fixed one of their wells at the school in the middle of the village which made everyone happy. I'm hoping that by working in this village and helping them get some water that I can decrease my chances of getting hijacked again on the road to Jebel Marra. A part of me is a bit wary though. I know these people need water too, but it's hard to get motivated to help them because I feel like they are responsible for this whole mess here in Darfur anyway. I dunno, sometimes I wish I could go bustin' in like ol' John Wayne and . . . well . . . you know!

I did have one cool thing happen to me today. Here's the story. . . . My favorite staff member is a man named Amir. He's muslim—nearly 90 percent of the folks here are—and he is the most eager to serve individual that I have ever met. Amir doesn't speak a lick of English, but somehow we've managed to become very close. I don't go anywhere without him. He was in Marla doing some work for me when it was bombed, and he was one of the guys they made get on his knees at gunpoint. So, I reckon we've been through a lot together. And still he goes with me everywhere, no matter how sketchy. He never complains and is always ready and willing to serve.

Last week we were in Jebel Marra. I was reading the bible and doing a lot of thinking about what I have done with what God has given me, etc., when Amir asked me about the book I was reading, and if I could get him one. Well, I came across a bible in Arabic and I gave it to him. I told him that I wanted him to have it so he could understand what and how I believe. He seemed excited but didn't say much about it. Then, today on the way to Melem, he told me through Hilary that he had been reading the bible, he said to me, "This book speaks truth." I was blown away.

Anyway, thanks y'all for all your prayers and support. If you don't know I finally was able to get the Wine to Water website up and going. So, if you get a chance check it out. It's pretty easy to remember: winetowater.org.

It is still a little bit in the works so if you see any grammatical errors, I'm sorry, I haven't had time to perfect it just yet.

Much Love,
Doc

TEN

~~~~~~~~~~~~~~~~~~

To say that Darfur is a challenging work environment is a gross understatement. The place is tough as nails. And it was burning out aid workers with the same kind of reckless abandon exhibited by the Janjaweed as they burned village after village across the sub-Sahara.

Cognizant of this epidemic, some aid organizations gave their workers mandatory six-month contracts. I'd also heard that UN workers were limited to twelve months. I had signed a one-year contract, and by March, just past my six-month anniversary in Darfur, we were already on our third Samaritan's Purse country director. They'd all either burned out, given up, or moved on to work in more desirable countries.

Last May, when I had asked Kenny Isaacs to send me to the worst place in the world, I had no idea that he'd pick so well—Darfur is it.

By this time, Andy was taking on a more managerial role in our offices. With the added responsibilities, he found himself staying up in Khartoum more and more, so Coy quickly filled the role as my copilot for hanging-out operations back at the compound.

Actually, since Coy didn't have an official job yet, I kept him busy working with my team doing pump rehabs in the field. It was partly selfish, because I really just enjoyed his company. We spent a lot of time talking and laughing on those long, dusty drives in the desert, and I soon realized that we were kindred spirits. Coy had a little bit of country boy in him, just like me. He loved shooting guns and rock and roll, and even played a mean guitar. Coy actually became the fourth member and lead guitarist in our little ragtag Darfur band.

"Brothas from a different motha!" we'd often profess in unison after a few shots of seeco were shared.

Over time, we also realized that we'd both been going through some tough patches in our lives back in the States. In fact, Coy eventually shared that a large part of the reason he was in Darfur was to get himself back together after his still-young marriage had imploded before his eyes.

"Dude, we should just box."

"What?" Coy asked.

"Let's box. Jonathan is on his R and R now, so we could

get him to bring us back a couple pairs of boxing gloves, and we can just beat the crap out of each other."

Coy listened intently, with a little glimmer in his blue eyes.

"It'd be good," I continued. "If we did it often enough we'd get into shape and work on some boxing skills, and we'd get a lot of aggression out."

It sounds silly, but boxing turned out to be exactly what we needed. Both of us were in serious need of therapy, and fisticuffs were, we thought, a serviceable substitute for a shrink. With that, the Darfur Fight Club was born.

We boxed most weekends. Usually it was just Coy and me fighting, though sometimes Jonathan took a turn. But never Andy. He was content just doing the live commentary. We absolutely tore into each other, trading blow after blow in those one-minute rounds. Some nights, usually after the seeco had been flowing, we'd drop the gloves and fight bare-knuckled. Those were the worst nights to wake up from.

One night in the spring, David Del Conte had a handful of his UN bosses in from New York staying at his compound, which happened to share an outside wall with ours. Well, that same night, we also had one of our rowdier boxing matches of the year. We even had some spectators, as a few fellow aid workers had joined us for drinks. The match was a doozy—we were absolutely going for it, while Andy, Jonathan, and the others howled wildly in appreciation.

The next morning as I left the compound, I ran into David and one of his houseguests.

"Are you the cause of all this commotion last night?" the well-dressed brunette said to me with a smile.

"Oh, yeah, sorry about that," I apologized. "I guess we got a little out of hand with the boxing."

"Boxing? I thought it was some kind of party going on."

"Nah, we were just making some ruckus boxing and cheering and whatever."

"David," she said, turning to Del Conte with a laugh. "How in the world did you swing getting to be neighbors with the only frat house in all of Nyala?"

Of course, life at our compound wasn't always fun and games. As Nyala's population swelled with more IDPs coming to town looking for food and work, so did the crime. Petty theft was rampant. And the break-ins in our neighborhood had become more brazen, with masked men even entering compounds at night while the occupants slept. Our neighbor across the street, a local physician, was actually stabbed to death in her sleep.

Going back to Nyala after being in the field was supposed to be a time for us to recoup. But my sleep began to suffer. I could no longer fully relax at night, and became so worried that our compound would be broken into that I slept with a knife and a club beside my bed. I realized I slept more soundly out in the field, so I dragged my bed outside into our courtyard and slept right there under our big lime tree. At least that way, I rationalized to myself, I wouldn't be trapped in my room, and I'd have a variety of escape routes if something were to happen. I wasn't used to being paranoid about my safety, but I couldn't help it.

From: Doc Hendley
To: Paul Wagner, Samaritan's Purse
Sent: Tuesday, March 22, 2005, 6:35:41 a.m.
Subject: This week's plan

Yo Paul,

This week I am planning on leaving early Wed. morning to begin rehabilitating the hand dug well in Hijar. I will leave the contractor there that night and then go to Sania Afandu to get the lorry and drop off Hamid. We need the lorry to pick up the cement and bricks that we aren't going to use in Rejeila. We will use them in Hijar now.

We will continue building latrines starting this week, I hope to get in 48 this month, that is 6 different sets of 8, not including what we do for the education team. This week Hamid will stay in Sania Afandu to help the latrines get started again, and he will start putting together a Hygiene promotion team. I will meet with the local sheikhs this week, where the latrines will go, and speak with them about having some women clean the latrines for free. I will do my best to put together a cleaning squad and a hygiene promotion squad strictly volunteer.

I will try to get these people to work in exchange for me putting in latrines, hand washing stations, etc. Because in the end it is to their benefit.

I will need money for:

Latrine supplies—50,000 SD

10 Hand washing bins—250,000 SD

Labor for latrines—35,000 SD

supplies for well rehab—75,000 SD

Labor for well rehab—70,000 SD

Total—480,000 SD

So it'd be great if you can bring $2,000 USD (that's about 500,000 SD). This will definitely keep us busy for at least two or three weeks' time.

thanks bro,

Doc

Having had good success with my visit to Melem, I wasn't super nervous about my next trip back up to Jebel Marra, but I was cautious. In particular, when we rounded that curve in the road where the Janjaweed had hijacked us, I started to get worried. I imagined I saw that same column of smoke rising from the hills, but there wasn't anything there. Actually, there wasn't anyone in the town of Kidingeer either, not even the regular SLA soldier outpost.

As we climbed the slow mountain road, my focus turned

to getting back up to Feina to see the sultan. In my truck I had packed shovels, axes, picks, and wheelbarrows that they could use to keep the road more passable. I hoped one day to get a well-drilling rig up to Feina, but as the roads stood now, there was little chance. So I was banking on the possibility that my donation of all those tools would be enough incentive to get the locals to work clearing the roads. We were also carrying a huge water bladder and supplies to get the locals set up with a bucket-chlorination project to start cleaning the water until I could get back up to drill some wells.

When we arrived in Feina, the sultan was meeting with a handful of SLA commanders, their machine guns resting carefully on the rugs beside them. But as soon as he saw us, the sultan stood and welcomed me warmly to sit with them for tea.

"He says he is happy you have decided to return," said Hilary. "But he wants to know why we haven't been back sooner. He thought—"

"Tell the sultan the reason we haven't been back," I said, interrupting Hilary, "is that we got hijacked by the Janjaweed."

The sultan looked a bit surprised as Hilary translated. The commanders mostly just nodded.

"Hilary, tell the commanders that it'd be very helpful if they could try to push the perimeter out a little farther and try to watch this area next time we're coming through, give us a little protection. And maybe if we called ahead when we're planning to come up they could tell us if they've had any Janjaweed sightings."

"This commander said yes, they'll definitely try to help, and will tell us if it's a good day to come or not," said Hilary.

"Good, good. And tell the sultan about all the tools in our truck. Tell him I want to get a rig up here to drill a well, but first they need to do something about these crazy roads. We've popped lots of tires on the way up here, even had a truck flip over. I can't bring a drill rig up here until they fix the roads."

"Yes, he says he understands."

"Excellent. Please tell him I'm glad to be back and that we'll come again soon with more supplies to get the bucket chlorination going."

The sultan and commanders all smiled in approval.

The following day, on our way back down the mountain in Kidingeer, our truck hit a large rock in the road and blew a tire. I was totally pissed, but had to laugh. We had no spare—because we'd actually used it to fix a flat on the way up to Feina the day before. I saw a small stand of shade trees up ahead where we could attempt to work on the tire. The Land Cruiser limped along until we reached the trees. At least there would be some relief from the heavy Darfur sun.

Hilary watched as Amir and I wrestled with the tire, when suddenly we were surrounded. Startled, I looked up, but was happy to recognize a couple of smiling faces among the group of SLA soldiers.

They were quick to help, waving me away from the tire.

Soon a pair of soldiers was working with Amir to knock the damaged tire off the rim, while other soldiers built a small fire and were busy melting rubber to patch our tire.

The rest of the soldiers in the unit, most of whom looked to be in their early twenties, sat cross-legged on the side of the road. They were smoking cigarettes and gambling on a game of cards. Every so often one of the soldiers would get up from the game and walk over to a young boy, offering him the last burning embers of a cigarette. The boy leaned coolly up against the hood of my Land Cruiser, watching the others work. He looked like a fourth grader, yet he wore the SLA uniform with the brim of his hat flipped up, and shouldered an AK-47 just like the others.

I had seen other boy soldiers, but what struck me was that he was the youngest I'd seen. And I felt oddly drawn to him. Maybe it was his deep gaze or his surprisingly hardened behavior as he casually sucked down the last few drags of a cigarette as if he'd been smoking since infancy. He seemed like a cool kid, but I had to remind myself that he'd probably killed more people than most grown men in our own military.

Still, I was intrigued. So I decided to go over and sit with the boy. I didn't say anything at first. I just sat down on the bumper next to him and watched the others fixing the tire.

Using my broken Arabic, I fumbled to ask his name and his age.

"*Ana* Mustafa," he answered. "*Ana Ithna 'ashar.*"

Twelve years old? When I was Mustafa's age, I lived for the weekend. All week long in school I would dream of Friday. And when it finally arrived, I'd be out in the woods behind my house, with my BB gun, pretending that I was in the midst of guerrilla warfare. Yet sitting there beside me was a child who wasn't pretending.

I did my best to make a joke—something, anything to coax a smile out of this young boy. Nothing worked, and he didn't seem very interested in talking either.

I had to learn the rest of his story. So I excused myself and sidled up to the commander of his unit while calling Hilary over for some translation help.

"That boy Mustafa, what's his story?" I asked, cutting right to the chase. "Where's he from?"

"The commander says Mustafa is from a small village on the western side of Jebel Marra," Hilary translated. "The Janjaweed destroyed his village and killed four of his family members when he was nine years old. But he escaped and joined the SLA to fight against the Janjaweed, and has been with us now for three years! Mustafa is young, but he is determined and hardworking. He is a good boy and a good soldier!"

The reality of Mustafa's childhood weighed heavily on me. I knew boy soldiers were commonplace in the SLA, but for the first time for me, I guess those boy soldiers finally had a face and a name. And it made me profoundly sad.

The men soon finished the tire repair, and I thanked them all for their good work and kindness. But I was reluctant to leave. I wanted to spend more time with Mustafa.

I hoped to see him again and decided I needed to give him a memento.

So I frantically dug through my bag, but all I could find was a necklace with a big canine tooth hanging from it. I had planned on giving it to Tasha as a souvenir, but it would have to do.

"Hilary, tell Mustafa I'm giving him this, but it's not a gift. It's a trade."

I pulled out the necklace and put it in his hand.

Mustafa's eyes lit up and, for a second, I saw the face of the twelve-year-old boy who was buried beneath the uniform and the gun.

"Tell him I'll be back, and that he needs to bring me something to trade for this necklace. And tell him he needs to stay safe so that he can keep up his part of the bargain."

With a big smile showing all his teeth, Mustafa replied, "*Tamam.*"

"The boy says okay! He'll do it. It's a deal."

I gave Mustafa a stiff handshake—his hand felt so small in mine—then made my way back to the truck, where my men waited eagerly. As we drove off I watched Mustafa and the other soldiers as they grew smaller in my rearview mirror. I wondered if I'd cross paths with that boy ever again.

From: Libbi Hendley
To: Doc Hendley
Sent: Sunday, March 20, 2005 10:05:42 p.m.
Subject: Mustafa

Hi Doc,

I just got back from Wilmington and read your latest email. It was incredible! I will be praying for Mustafa. That child has the saddest face! Does he have any family left? He has never had a childhood! He has not been free to play war, because he has been in one! He has not been able to be carefree, and not have to worry about where he will sleep at night and if he will wake up in the morning. He has not had a mother have a hot meal on the table ready for him when he comes in from playing. He has not been able to go to school or to soccer practice. He has not been able to go to sleep in a clean bed and wake up and eat breakfast and put on clean clothes in the morning. He has not had parents to pray with him at night. He has not had friends to go fishing with and not worry if they throw them back because they will still be able to come home and eat. I could go on and on. I can't get his sad face out of my mind.

I'm glad that a lot of people sent you emails for

your birthday. I hope you know that you are loved and missed.

    I am thankful for you,
    Mom

-----Original Message-----

"Doc Hendley" wrote:

Subject: Warning! It's a long one.

I was lying out under the stars in Jebel Marra (the Montana of Sudan) when I started writing down what I was going to write in this next e-mail. So y'all bear with me on this one, 'cause it might have some feelings and crap in it. Now, I normally don't like to share feelings with anyone other than my dog or a beer, but I need to make an exception this time, 'cause there are some things I gotta say.

Whenever I lie awake like this at night and I ask the Lord to speak to me, I am usually brought back to one question. . . . That question is, "What have you done with what I have given you?" Tonight, when asked this question, I began to first think about what specific things the Lord has given me. I was able to boil everything down to the two most important things in my life: my family and friends.

I met a boy soldier the other day. His name is Mustafa. He's now twelve years old and has been fighting with the rebels since he was nine. Four of his family have been killed by the Janjaweed, and now fighting is his life.

Meeting that boy made me think even more about all that I have to be thankful for. I love my family more than anything on this earth, and I know that in that sense I have not taken for granted what God has given me. The same is true with my friends. Some of you I haven't even known very long, and I know without a doubt that you would risk your neck to save mine, and I am sure y'all know that I would do the same for you.

I know no one is perfect, but if I ever get out of this place I'm gonna make sure that I'm a better son, brother, and friend to all of you. And I ain't gettin' all mushy just because it's nighttime and I am alone under the stars. I guess I wanted to say these things because being here makes me aware of my mortality. Being here makes me know that at any moment, if the Lord so wills, I could be gone. Thinking about that tonight is what made me write this letter. I wish I could write one letter to everyone separately so I could be more specific about what each one of you means to me. But I can't, or just not right now, 'cause I would be in front of the computer for weeks.

I don't really know what all this stuff means. I don't know what God has in store for my life here, and after. But I do know one thing: Whatever it is, I ain't gonna turn into some wuss who talks all proper, and combs his hair nice, and never messes up, and only listens to public radio, and . . . well, I guess I could go on and on, but y'all get the point.

Whew! I am in Nyala now, and I was trying to decide whether I was gonna type and send what I wrote. These past few days I've had to drive through the area where I was hijacked, so the insecurity may have added a little to the letter. But in the end I decided to send it because the things I was thinking and feeling are things that are true. I reckon in this world there is so much that is uncertain and so much that is fake or not true. So when I think or feel something that I know for certain to be true it can never be a bad thing to share it with the people I love.

Just don't go thinking that these types of letters are gonna come around often, because they ain't. And don't go thinking that when I get back I'm gonna wanna talk about my "feelings" and all that!

I love all y'all,
Doc

ELEVEN

At a UN security meeting in late March, David Del Conte mentioned a region in northern Jebel Marra, on the other side of the mountain range and deep within a UN no-go zone, that was still untouched by any sort of aid operations. The main village there is named Leiba, and I decided my team needed to get up there.

So I had Ismael ready the trucks and load the Buffalo with a bunch of boxes of chlorine tablets. The plan was to head up to Leiba, do an assessment of their water needs, and then swing back through Feina, where we'd drop off the chlorine tabs with the sultan so we could get the bucket-chlorination program rolling there.

Waheed rode in the Buffalo with me, chain-smoking his Bringi cigarettes like always. He was a mild-mannered teacher in his mid-forties from Jebel Marra who had been working hard with Andy on some school projects. But Andy wasn't using Waheed that week, so I snatched him up to accompany me, because he had deep ties with the SLA and spoke excellent English. Ismael followed us in the other Land Cruiser with one of our drivers named Mohamed.

Amir wanted to join us but he was bedridden, battling a serious bout of malaria. Before we left I stopped by to visit him and bring him his week's wages and some extra money to buy more medicine. When he found out we were headed back to Jebel Marra again he was upset that he couldn't come. Amir was one of my most loyal workers and, I believe, felt it was his duty to help protect me. In fact, before he'd let me leave, he pulled the string of hijabs off his arm and handed them to me. These small brown cubes are actually rolled-up pieces of the Koran blessed by a local medicine man. Locals believed that each hijab would ward off a single bullet. Amir had seven hijabs on his string, and it was like his own personal shield. True hijabs like those, not the fake ones I'd seen hawked in the local markets, are extremely valuable. Amir probably paid the equivalent of five days' labor for his string of seven. Locals believed in them wholeheartedly, and Amir insisted I bring it with me to Jebel Marra. While I obviously didn't have faith in the power of the hijabs, Amir's gesture was overwhelming.

After passing through Kidingeer, our two-truck convoy

looped northwest around the mountain and we slowly picked our way up the rocky dirt path that passes for a major road in this part of Darfur. An hour later we pulled into Leiba, a small village that looked like a set straight out of an old spaghetti western movie, and similar to so many other villages we'd visited in Darfur. There was a single dusty main street with a couple shops, an empty market, and an SLA outpost. Mud huts pocked the green hills surrounding town, home to the two thousand residents of Leiba.

We drove along slowly, looking for someone to talk to, but it wasn't a market day, so the town was quiet. I parked our truck smack in the middle of town and we hopped out for a look.

Almost immediately armed SLA soldiers began appearing from around corners of buildings, and within seconds we were surrounded on all sides.

I was actually pleased to see these guys. The SLA had always been very hospitable to us, since we'd made a name for ourselves as really helping their people. But something seemed different this time. Instead of greeting us warmly, these guys seemed unusually skittish.

"Waheed, ask them if Commander Mohamed Isa called this morning to inform them we were coming."

"Doc, they say no one called ahead," said Waheed. "They want to take us to their outpost until they can verify things with their commanders. They want to detain us."

"What?" I said incredulously while whipping out my sat

phone. "Tell them I have the numbers of all their command-ers right here in my phone."

"Doc, they're insisting we follow them back to their out-post. They say it's just down this main street."

"Okay, but this is bullshit. I'm gonna get someone on the phone and they'll take care of it."

The soldiers were relatively polite as they escorted the four of us to a small brick building beside the outpost. The youngest soldier swung open the sheet-metal door and ges-tured for us all to enter the dark, dirt-floored room. That was when it hit me—they were putting us in jail.

"Waheed, tell them this ain't cool!" I growled. I picked up my Thuraya and started dialing more commanders' num-bers, but my sat phone wouldn't get service inside the low-slung building.

I felt like punching myself in the face. This was the first time I hadn't done all my due diligence. I just assumed these people knew who I was and were expecting us. But the sec-ond I got overly confident was the second I got thrown in jail. The SLA had imprisoned a fair number of aid workers in the past, and I knew full well that some were held for weeks and months at a time. Some were even killed by their captors.

After some careful translation with Waheed, the guard let me out of the cell to try to make more calls. For two hours, in and out of the cell I went, trying in vain to reach any of my key SLA contacts. The Thuraya network appeared to be down, but eventually I got through to Mohamed Isa on my Iridium phone.

"*A salam alaikum*, Commander Isa. *Ana* Doc with *moya*—the water guy."

"*Nam nam*, Doc. *Keif?*" he said warmly. "How you are?"

"Not good. One minute, sir, one minute," I say, motioning Waheed out of the cell and handing the phone to him. "Waheed, tell him what's up."

Waheed spoke in quick, spirited Arabic and soon handed the phone to the guard. His eyes instantly grew larger as he spoke with the commander. He immediately waved over a couple others, and in a matter of minutes, everything was sorted out. We were all released and they proceeded to roll out the red carpet for us.

"*Malesh, malesh,*" said one soldier, bowing slightly to me, embarrassed.

"He says they are very sorry," translated Waheed. "There was some miscommunication. These soldiers and the town are very happy to welcome us now. They are very sorry."

Before long the sheikh had been summoned and we were escorted around town on a guided tour. A rowdy trail of children followed us as we walked, surveying the area and checking out a series of primitive hand-dug wells near a dried-up wadi. I took notes and mentally cataloged all of the things that we could do to help the villagers. First we'd work to reinforce the walls of the wells with concrete, eventually capping the open wells and installing new hand pumps. This would be the best way to ensure that the water in those wells remained clean and protected from the environment—and from the Janjaweed, who had recently taken to tossing dead animals, even human remains, down wells to contaminate them at the source. God willing, we'd soon find a way to get a drill rig up this mountain and start drilling proper wells all over the region.

We chatted with the sheikh as we strolled back to the main street to join the village elders for a special dinner to celebrate our visit to Leiba, but our conversation was interrupted by the rumble and roar of an SLA lorry. It was a large dark-blue cargo truck with four-foot-tall wooden slats lining its bed, which was packed with about twenty armed soldiers, their jellabiyas and head wraps covered in rust-colored sand and dust.

As the soldiers piled out, it was obvious they were exhausted. Some were limping, and a pair looked badly injured. One young man in his early twenties, holding his left arm, which was covered in dark red blood, came stumbling toward me, looking in my eyes with a helpless gaze. I didn't recognize this man, or any other of the soldiers, for that matter, but it soon became clear that they knew exactly who I was.

"This man says can you help him. He says you are a doctor and he needs you to fix his wound."

"Waheed, tell him I ain't that kind of doc!" I said with an uncomfortable laugh. "Ismael, run and get the medical kit out of my truck. Waheed, can you ask this guy who's in charge here? Who's the commander? We need to figure out what the hell happened here."

With his bloody hand, the soldier pointed at an older man in uniform, now leaning against the outpost clutching his leg, which was wildly swollen from the knee down. There was no definition—no way of telling where his ankle or calf began or ended. It was gross, but I couldn't help staring at his leg as the man described the bloody firefight they'd just had with the Janjaweed in the village of Teige, forty miles to the southeast.

Apparently, a week earlier the Janjaweed had kidnapped and raped a pair of young girls from Leiba, and the soldiers went to Teige looking for those girls—and a little vengeance. Unfortunately this wasn't a rare incident. As if it wasn't bad enough that the Janjaweed burned entire villages, looted whatever they pleased, and killed villagers, tossing dead bodies into their wells to ensure the water would be forever contaminated, the Janjaweed also regularly raped the women and children of SLA villages. I couldn't blame these soldiers for risking their lives to avenge the heinous crimes against their women. Those kinds of stories even made me yearn to kill a bunch of Janjaweed myself.

Although I've had very little medical training beyond basic first aid, I was pretty sure I could give these soldiers better care than they'd receive from local medicine men, whose typical treatment consisted of packing bullet wounds with an infection-inducing mix of mud and ash.

As I surveyed the young man's wound, it became clear that

the bullet had made a clean exit, passing straight through the meat of his forearm. I used a pair of shiny forceps to tightly grip iodine-soaked gauze as I scrubbed out the wound, penetrating the hole as deeply as I could. Then I flushed it with iodine and covered the entry and exit and wrapped his arm with a bandage. The young soldier barely winced as I fumbled to clean and dress his wound. It was as if he'd done all of this before. And he probably had.

While the others worked on the commander's leg, I made a call back to Samaritan's Purse headquarters in Nyala—as was protocol whenever we witnessed or heard about nearby fighting or insecurities. Andy answered the phone and I quickly described the situation to him.

"Listen, Andy, I think I'm just going to park my butt here in Leiba for a week or so and do some more assessments in the area while we let the fighting die down a little."

Andy was very concerned.

"Nah, I ain't worried," I responded. "Teige is a good way away. I just wanted to give you a heads-up about what happened, and so you could have David pass it along at the next OCHA meeting."

Andy agreed and asked me to call back later that night to check back in after he had a chance to download the info to the Samaritan's Purse country director.

The villagers threw a big celebration for us that night. We all hung out in the sheikh's compound. Rather than a small mud hut, the sheikh's home was a large rock structure fenced

in with thick briar bushes on top of a low rock-wall structure. There we enjoyed a meal of goat that they slaughtered
just for us. There was plenty of fool, and big bowls of aseeda,
basically a huge dome-shaped ball of dough in stringy brown
gravy. We all sat together near the campfire, digging our bare
hands into these bowls of food. No one uses utensils in Darfur. It was kind of fun eating that way, but it was totally
unhygienic, and no doubt the source of many stomach ailments that plagued me throughout my time there.

They served more tea after dinner. About this time the
sheikh had someone bring out a low rope bed for me to
sit on. It felt nice to get up off the cold sand. Ismael was sitting on the ground nearby, so I gestured for him to bring his
tea over and join me.

"Good dinner, huh?"

"Yes, Mr. Doc. Very nice. Thank you."

Amir had always been my right-hand man, but as we
got busier and my team grew I started to find myself in the
field with Ismael more often. Like Amir, Ismael was a tireless
worker. He was eternally grateful to me for giving him a job,
but he wasn't quite as subservient as Amir. Ismael carried
himself with slightly more confidence, and he spoke pretty
good English.

As the campfire crackled, I learned that Ismael had a wife
and three children living in a small village about a half day's
drive from Nyala. Every week after working with us, Ismael
rode the bus back home to deliver his wages to his family.

Realizing that he was such a dedicated family man made me respect Ismael even more.

"How many children do you have, Mr. Doc?"

"I don't have any children, Ismael. I'm not married."

With that Ismael shot me a puzzled look. In the Muslim culture of Darfur, the only reason a man is not married is because he's still working to save up enough money for the dowry needed to buy a wife. If a man already had enough to afford the cows, goats, and sheep a woman's father would demand, then that man would most certainly already have a wife. This is every man's life goal. The thought of being single and playing the field is an entirely foreign concept to these guys.

"I don't understand. Why aren't you married?"

"Well, I don't know, Ismael. That's actually a good question."

And I didn't have a good answer for Ismael. It made me stop to think. Back home in the States, the "playing the field" line always seemed to be the perfect knee-jerk answer to questions like this, but for the first time it just didn't feel like enough.

"I don't know how to explain it, Ismael. Sorry."

Before turning in for the night, I stepped outside the compound to call Andy. As I raised the antenna on my sat phone, I stopped for a moment to marvel at the night sky. It reminded me again of those times I spent camping out on the ranch in Montana. I'd stay up late into the night just staring at the sky, scanning the horizon for shooting stars, and not wanting to close my eyes for fear I'd miss one streaking across the heavens.

"I'm glad you called, Doc. I actually just got off the phone with the regional director. He says they want you guys back in Nyala immediately," explained Andy.

"Man, Andy, I don't think that's such a good idea. The SLA are telling me the road home is full of Janjaweed right now. They're telling me it's not safe."

"I totally understand, Doc. I'm just telling you what the boss man is saying. Whenever there's fighting in the area, you're required to return to headquarters immediately—it's just protocol."

"Well, protocol sucks. This just ain't right."

"They already talked to the AU. They said they'll make a sweep of the road early tomorrow morning. They'll have the road cleared for you."

"These SLA dudes are telling me otherwise. And they've got bullet wounds to prove it. I don't know, man."

"I hear what you're saying, Doc."

"I guess I'll just sleep on it and call you in the morning to tell you what I decide to do."

"Cool, man. Talk to you then."

By the time I got back to my bed, which someone had neatly arranged for me right next to the dwindling campfire, my head was spinning. Should I follow the rules and come home, even if it meant getting my ass shot up? Or should

I listen to the SLA and stay up there in the mountains, even if it meant losing my job? I had never been one for following the rules to a T. But lately I was beginning to think maybe I should start.

I reached down and grabbed my backpack to fish out a small care package that arrived earlier in the week from my family. There was a handful of cigars from Mom, plus quite a few notes and cards, including a handwritten letter from my granddaddy Dick. I lit a cigar and carefully opened the envelope—only one other time in my life had I received a letter from Dick.

> *Hi Dickson,*
>
> *This is your buddy and good friend, Dick. We've all missed you around.*
> *You looked good in the pictures you sent home. You looked tough as Rambo, but don't try to be a Rambo. I pray for your team every day. I pray that you'll watch your back, front, side when you are out doing your work or visiting. I pray that you will be careful. Take no chances, and protect yourself.*
> *I was glad to see you with those people in the picture. I hope they are your friends so they can protect you.*
> *Dickson, I pray that you and your team are successful in your daily duties (fresh water, food, and the word of*

the Lord Jesus Christ to all the people you meet and who are around).

Dickson, I feel good. My balance is not so good, but I am healthy and I thank God for my health. Lucille and I went to see your mom and dad in Boone. That is a wonderful house they have, a beautiful place to live.

I am not much of a letter writer but all I know is that I'm proud of you. It takes a man to do what you are doing. To do God's work, Dickson, you are a brave man. I pray that God will bless you and protect you and bring you home safe.

Love you,
Dick

TWELVE

~~~~~~~~~~~~~~~~

You know the kind of morning when you wake up and have that unmistakable feeling that all is right with the world? Well, this was just such a morning.

I walked out of the sheikh's compound refreshed from a good night's rest and paused to drink in the view. To my west, the rich morning light painted the Jebel Marra mountains with sunny hues of gold and copper, covered in a light, gauzy mist. I watched as the women of the village slowly walked up into the terraced fields to tend the sorghum and sun-dried tomatoes. To my east, the land fell sharply to the sub-Saharan desert below. Down there, the world looked in-hospitable. Blazing hot and bone-dry.

An older, sweet-faced woman found me by my Land Cruiser to deliver my morning tea. I turned to thank her but was suddenly face-to-face with the young soldier I'd treated the night before. He looked at me sheepishly, gesturing toward his injured arm. I changed his bandages—the wound looked like it was actually beginning to heal—but I implored him to keep it clean.

"Shukoran geezera, shukoran geezera," he said, thanking me warmly.

After fixing his bandage I suddenly remembered I'd promised to get back in touch with Andy about whether or not we'd be returning to Nyala right away. So I fired up the sat phone again.

"Good morning, Andy. So what's the deal? Did you hear anything?"

"Yeah, actually just talked with the AU. They said they did a sweep of the road to Nyala this morning," Andy ex-plained. "They said it's all clear. You're good to go."

"What do you mean, we're good to go?"

"The AU did a sweep. They said they even met with the locals in Teige, and the villagers all said there hadn't been any fighting around there."

"Really? That's kind of funny, because I literally just fin-ished changing the bloody bandage on an SLA soldier who says Teige is where he got shot just yesterday. And don't you know that neither the SLA nor the Janjaweed are ever honest with the AU? No one trusts them—not even the bad guys."

"I know, Doc. I hear you. That's just what they're saying to me. And I'm just relaying what the boss man told me to tell you. They said the road is clear, and to have you get back here immediately."

"All right. Fine. I understand, man. I'll figure it out."

I hung up and grabbed Waheed. Together we found the SLA commander with the busted-up leg and joined him as he sipped his morning tea. He was the oldest of the soldiers, in his late thirties, and his camo fatigues fit slightly tightly around his chubby belly. As usual in Sudan, the guys who were in charge always seemed to have the most fat on their bones, because they got the largest servings at mealtimes.

He was polite but stone-faced and emotionless. All I could think of was, *This man is what a boy soldier like Mustafa turns into after twenty years of fighting.*

I had Waheed ask the commander what he'd recommend we do, and if he thought the road back to Nyala was safe enough to travel.

"He says no, no, it's not safe," translated Waheed. "He says we should not go back that way today."

"Damn, that's what I was afraid of," I replied.

"But if we do decide to go back to Nyala, he says his troops can escort us as far as Kidingeer. But they aren't prepared to go any farther—that's all Janjaweed and GoS (government of Sudan) territory now."

Every cell in my body was telling me to stay in Jebel Marra. The beautiful golden mountains looked so enticing. It was where I wanted to be, where I wanted to be doing my water work. But my brain's rule-abiding side, no matter how small, won the battle. I decided to follow my boss's wishes and do exactly as I was told. For once.

"Okay, so if your guys can escort us to Kidingeer, we'll part ways there and continue on to Nyala."

As Waheed translated this to the commander, his face morphed from stone to a smirk. Waheed didn't have to translate the face. It was clear he was saying, *All righty, young man, suit yourself. And don't say I didn't warn you.*

We packed up our gear immediately, bade farewell to the sheikh, and, around noon, hopped into our trucks for the drive home to Nyala. Just as promised, the commander and his soldiers escorted us all the way to Kidingeer. There were probably eight of them, mostly the younger soldiers, piled atop a dusty dark-blue Land Cruiser. The truck's roof and windshield had been chopped off, and in their place sat a fifty-caliber machine gun mounted on the hood near the passenger side. It was the classic SLA battle truck, and odds were that it was stolen. Both the SLA and the Janjaweed were well-known for hijacking aid workers and stealing their fresh white Land Cruisers. We'd yet to lose a truck, so I figured we must've been doing something right—or at least something different.

As we pulled into Kidingeer, our SLA escort peeled off to

the side of the road and waved us on our way. But I parked the truck, and Waheed and I hopped out to say good-bye.

"The commander says if we have any trouble to give him a call on his sat phone."

I pulled out my well-worn, leather-bound notepad, where I kept all the names and numbers of key people I met.

"He says they'll do what they can if we need any help on the way home."

"*Shukoran,*" I said gratefully.

I shoved the Land Cruiser into drive and we veered along the road to the east. In the rearview mirror, I watched as the soldiers slowly disappeared.

Forty-five dusty, bumpy minutes later we reached Teige.

As we rumbled deeper into the village, something caught my eye on the side of the road. About a hundred yards up on the left, I saw a man crouched down. He was dressed in the traditional garb of Arabian nomads, a once-white but now-dirty yellowish-brown flowing jellabiya with half his face covered in an equally dirty white head wrap.

After spending nine months working in Darfur, I'd grown accustomed to the occasional roadblock, where SLA rebels or Janjaweed fighters would put their hands out and guns in the air, firing a warning shot. Then I'd drop the name of a local commander or tribal leader to convince them to let us pass. But this time there was no one blocking the road.

We were traveling about thirty mph, so we came upon him quickly. Fifty feet. Forty feet. Twenty feet. As we closed in on the man I clearly saw the barrel of his AK-47 tracking our progress. It felt as though his gun was aimed directly at my face. I also noticed a half dozen other men, some wearing the green camouflage fatigues of the Sudanese army, crouching along either side of the road nearby. All of their weapons were trained directly on us.

Do I keep going? Do I slow down? I asked myself.

My gut answered first and I floored the Buffalo. She lurched and groaned in response, kicking a thick cloud of dust into the air. As soon as our truck was passing the first man, almost exactly perpendicular with him, I watched as he squeezed the trigger.

From: Doc Hendley

To: Jeff Hendley

Sent: Thursday, April 7, 2005, 11:16:06 p.m.

Subject: The D.L. on the incident

Well, I reckon all y'all wanna know the story. And I don't really know what I am supposed to say. . . . But you know what, I don't care anymore. I've tried to keep politically sensitive issues out of most of my communication, and all that got me was a couple of trucks full of lead from machine gun fire, so I reckon I'm sick of playing the political game.

This whole incident started on April 5th. I went
to a new area in Jebel Marra called Leiba to do an
assessment to see if the people there were in need of
food and water, etc. While I was there trying to make
friends with the local rebel group, a lorry with rebels
from Kidingeer (another area that I work in) pulled up.
I hung out with them for a bit and found out that they
had just come from a village called Teige. Two days prior
they heard that 2 young girls were kidnapped by the
Janjaweed and raped in Teige, so they went to regulate
the situation. Well, more Janjaweed ended up being in
the area than they thought. As a result, this one truck full
wasn't enough for them to fight very long so they were
forced to retreat. They retreated to Leiba, where they ran
into me. They only had two injured out of the 15 or so
in the truck, one was shot through the arm and one had
a busted up leg. SO, I took this opportunity to put my
nickname to use. I got our medical kit out of the truck
and proceeded to play "Doc" on this dude with the hole
in his arm, and I must say I think I did a pretty dadburn
good job too.

Anyway, I hung around these rebels most of that
night because I wanted to change the wounded man's
bandages a few times before he left. While we were
together they clued me in on the situation and told me
that the road out was not safe and to wait till they could

patrol it before I moved. So, I made the call back to the office in Nyala, and they, of course, contacted the AU.

The next morning, April 6, the AU did an "assessment" of the road in Teige and said that there were no problems; in fact, they said that they spoke with a lot of people who said there was never any fighting at all. It's funny, I was told this just after changing the wounded soldier's bandage one last time. Anyway, we were told that the road was clear and that we could drive it.

So, I was instructed to come on back to Nyala to try and let things blow over. I was reluctant to go, because the SLA (the Rebels) told me that they patrolled the road surrounding Jebel Marra, and it was safe to travel to the other areas that I needed to go on the assessment, but they said they weren't sure about the road to Teige, where the fighting took place, which also happens to be the only road back to Nyala. So, they just told me to be careful if I had to travel it and call them on their SAT phones if I needed anything. These guys are just awesome.

Well, we reached Teige, and that's when stuff started to hit the fan. I didn't really have a chance to call the SLA for back-up, I was just trying to make it out alive. Right when our two-truck convoy entered Teige, we were ambushed. I made eye contact with the guy who fired the first shot. It was surreal staring down his barrel as it followed me and then seeing the chamber burst out a round. He was close. I had my window down, so not only was it loud but I could feel the shock from the blast. I don't know why that bullet didn't hit me. . . . After this first blast the whole place erupted in machine gun fire and when the bullets started smashing the rear window and banging around in the truck I ducked my head and drove with my eyes barely above the dashboard so I wouldn't be hit in the head. I felt like I was in the movie *Saving Private Ryan* when they were getting shot at on the beach.

This wasn't a few pop shots. These men were shooting to kill. And only God knows why there were no casualties. All together in this place we estimated between 30 to 40 Janjaweed. Of these, around eight were in position to ambush our convoy. All eight were firing their machine guns heavily at our vehicles. I'll never forget what bullets sound like tearing through sheet metal and whizzing by in the air. . . .

I was worried about the truck behind me but I didn't stop to see if they were okay for a few miles. But they also miraculously made it out alive. They were moving slowly 'cause the front left tire had been shot out. I instructed them to drive on the flat for another few kilometers and then we changed the tire like we were at Daytona Speedway. I couldn't contact anyone at the office, so I began calling random numbers. I finally got through to one of my friends at UN OCHA, who gave me some good advice about what to do from there.

I am going to leave the rest of the story out 'cause it mostly deals with an interview with the AU. It is probably best to leave that part out anyway, because I am still angry with the AU and I might say something that will disappoint momma.

Y'all, I have said it before and I will say it again. I am convinced that your faithful prayers, and the good Lord's will, are the only reasons that I am still alive to write you this letter. Thank you so much. I am indebted to each one of you for your faithfulness.

I'll be in touch. I love y'all.
Doc

THIRTEEN

USAID

DARFUR—Humanitarian Emergency
Fact Sheet #28, Fiscal Year (FY) 2005
April 8, 2005

Security

According to the USAID Disaster Assistance Response
Team (USAID/DART), on April 6, a two-vehicle non-
governmental organization (NGO) humanitarian convoy
was fired upon near Teige, approximately 7 km west of

Mershing, South Darfur. The lead vehicle was hit three
times and the second vehicle was hit twice and received
a flat tire. No one was injured.

Ever since the ambush I guess I started acting differently.
I wasn't sure at first if anyone else could tell, but I definitely
felt different. I became reclusive. Quiet. Angry. Confused.
Sad. Depressed. Nervous. Fricking pissed. It was a tsunami of
emotion.

I was sick of eating canned tuna and day-old fool. I was
tired of having yet another new Samaritan's Purse country
director to answer to every month—was that job a revolv-
ing door?—and they hadn't even bothered to call about the
ambush yet. I was pissed that everything I tried to do, almost
every water project I put into motion, was eventually ruined
by the Janjaweed. What had I even accomplished in the
more than nine months I'd been in Sudan?

I didn't know who to trust anymore. I was feeling a little
paranoid. I felt like the Janjaweed, the GoS, and the local
police were all in cahoots. Then sometimes when I saw GoS
soldiers or police patrolling the streets of Nyala, I had this
overwhelming desire to walk up and smash them in the face.
It came over me like a wave. Naturally, striking a man in the
face who is carrying an AK-47 is not an intelligent thing to
do. But that was how I felt.

Turned out I wasn't fooling anyone. Andy and Coy were onto me.

"Dude, you need to get yourself together, Doc," said Andy. "You're gonna get yourself killed out there acting like this. Or you're gonna kill somebody."

He was probably right. I needed to get back to normal. Or if not normal, at least back to where I'd been the day before we got ambushed. I just didn't know how to get there.

One afternoon while I sat alone in my room at the compound listening to Ray LaMontagne's album *Trouble* over and over again, there was a knock.

Coy gingerly cracked open my wooden door.

"Doc, some guy's here to see you."

I looked up and the door opened fully to reveal a man dressed in khakis and a white short-sleeved polo with the Red Cross logo embroidered on his left chest. He must've been in his early thirties, tall, with short dark-blond hair and small round John Lennon glasses.

"My name's Marcus."

I just nodded.

As soon as he spoke, I figured he was a Swede, a veteran aid worker. Probably a lifer.

"You're the one who got ambushed, right?" he asked. "I read the report last week. Then I heard you were still in town and I wanted to come by and see you."

Another nod.

"So why are you still here?"

Silence.

"When something only half this bad happens to someone from the Red Cross, our headquarters pulls that person out. Puts them on temporary leave."

"To tell you the truth, I don't know why I'm still here," I eventually volunteered. "I guess I'm still just processing it."

This time Marcus was qzuiet. He just nodded.

"That first bullet should have smashed me in the face," I continued. "So why the hell am I still alive?"

I wasn't sure why this man was there, standing in my room. But I could tell he was a good guy. And it seemed like he genuinely cared.

"Man, it's okay. The way you're feeling—it's completely normal," he replied warmly. "If your organization lets you, you should definitely take a break. Get out of Sudan for a bit. You can't be of much value to the people you're trying to help when you're troubled."

That was pretty much it. I thanked him for coming by, we shook hands, and he was gone. Never even caught his last name. Never saw him again.

I'm not sure if Andy overheard our conversation or if the Swede talked to him before leaving, but the very next morn- ing he told me I needed to take a break and go to Khartoum for a few days.

"Doc, I still haven't heard from anybody in Boone about

what to do about things. So I'm telling you, as interim Darfur head dude, or whatever the hell I am right now, you need to get out of here. Go to Khartoum. Leave today."

If he had told me to go a day earlier, I probably would have protested. Maybe it was the Swede. Maybe I just finally realized I needed to get out of Nyala. But I left.

I found Khartoum as hot and dusty as ever.

Though there were a number of steel-and-glass buildings sprouting up throughout the city (courtesy of that dirty oil money from China), in general, Khartoum was still much like Nyala, with its dust-covered, sand-colored buildings rising from the Sahara. There were tons of lumbering old donkey carts and loud tuk tuks zipping around the streets. With a population of nearly five million, Khartoum was just a regular Darfuri village masquerading as a large cosmopolitan city. It was as if those five million folks were busy simply going about their day-to-day lives, seemingly unaware of the horrors happening in the desert to their west.

Around midday the following day, I arrived at the Samaritan's Purse country office in Khartoum. Housed in a six-story modern office building, Samaritan's Purse occupied the bottom floor, with a large office area and a guesthouse that was popular with aid workers from various organizations.

Though there were plenty of people to interact with, I mostly kept to myself. My favorite thing was to take the stairs up to the building's roof, where I could look out over the city. I'd sit up there alone, puffing a cigar.

Khartoum was always alive with noise, the steady hum of a city punctuated by taxis honking like crazy and the loud whine of the tuk tuks. It wasn't a clean place, but it still mostly just smelled like dust. The stuff covered everything, courtesy of huge dust storms that could turn the day into night within minutes.

My second-favorite thing to do was to close myself up inside my guesthouse room, crank the air conditioner, and pretend I was somewhere else besides Sudan. I'd just wrap up in all of the covers and blankets and fall asleep, cozy and content.

One evening, a call finally came through from Samaritan's Purse headquarters. It was the new international projects director, the guy who recently replaced Kenny Issacs, who had left the organization to take a job with the United States Agency for International Development (USAID). The man on the other end of the line apologized for taking so long to respond to my situation, and said he'd arranged for me to travel to Kenya, where a Christian counselor was waiting to talk with me.

I was pretty damn sure I didn't want a thing to do with any Christian counselor. But two weeks away from Darfur, with air-conditioning, a hotel bed, and cold beer? Sign me up.

From: Doc Hendley
To: Jeff Hendley
Sent: Friday, April 15, 2005, 6:57:22 a.m.
Subject: "Hi didily ho, neighbors" (Flanders)

My folks told me that some people have been asking
how I'm holding up and where I am, etc. So, I figured I'd
give y'all an update.

Well, this past weekend the guys in Darfur told me
to get the heck out of there and go to Khartoum to take
a break. I was reluctant to go, because I hadn't heard
anything from my bosses, but they pushed me enough to
where I gave in . . . It wasn't too hard to give in 'cause I
wanted to get away from that place for a while anyway.

So, I took off to Khartoum. When I was there I finally
got word from one of my bosses. He told me that he
wanted to send me to Nairobi for two weeks to get out of
Sudan. He said I needed to be debriefed and also said he
wanted me to "talk" to someone about what all happened
and how I was doing. I, of course, was excited to leave
Sudan for a couple weeks, but I was a little nervous about
what he meant by "talk" to someone. I hate the word
"talk." When I hear it I feel like I did when I was 5 and my
mom wanted me to take my cough medicine. I actually
think I gag a little bit even now when I hear "you need to
talk" or even *much, much* worse "we need to talk" . . .

Sorry, I had to stop writing 'cause I think I threw up a little in my mouth. Anyway, so while I was thinking about the beautiful crime filled city of Nai-robbery, in the back of my mind I was picturing myself lying on a couch talking to some dude about when I was seven and I dropped my "Rainbow Rocket Pop" in the dirt and I couldn't get another one 'cause the ice cream man had already driven away.

But, now I'm here and so far it looks like this is just a chance for me to relax. I haven't seen any shrinks around, or any kind of Christian Counselor (which would be infinitely worse than a shrink 'cause it would be like being stuck in a room with Flanders from the Simpsons. I can just hear it now. . . . "Hi didily ho, Dickson, I hear someone's feeling a tid biddily on the joyfully challenged side.")

Wait . . . Wait . . . I think I just threw up in my mouth again . . . Regardless, any of y'all who know me know that I am beyond repair by a shrink or a Flanders. I mean it would take years of intensive shock therapy to get me back to a normal state of mind.

So, to answer everyone's questions of how I'm holding up, I am doing great. I have an appointment for a deep tissue massage at 3:00 . . . (no Gerry, not that kind of massage) and well, those of you who know me know that I will find plenty of ways to chill out and relax in a non-Muslim country. Thank y'all so much for all your e-mails of support. They were all great. I got anywhere from mushy ones like "stay strong, I love you," etc., to ones that made me laugh like "that's what happens when you mess with those African chiefs' daughters."

Y'all, I am so grateful that I have such a faithful group of people back home praying for me and my team. I love y'all. I will leave with a quote that my friend Sheri Baker sent me. It's by Winston Churchill, he had a rough time in Africa as well. . . .

"There is nothing more exhilarating than to be shot at and missed."

Much Love,
Doc

I did eventually sit down with that Christian counselor. And while he was a good dude, I was, admittedly, not very cooperative. I didn't say much at all. I didn't give him much to work with, but he did manage to get me thinking.

"Doc, I feel like there's something else going on here," he said. "Maybe there's another reason you're so upset, something in addition to the ambush. Just think about it."

After about two weeks in Nairobi and a grand total of sixty minutes in counseling, I returned to Nyala. I hadn't been cured, but I knew I needed to get back with Amir, Hilary, Ismael, and the rest of my team. I needed to get back into the field.

My second night home in Nyala, Coy and I worked on a jar of seeco and boxed late into the night. There were no spectators. Andy was in Khartoum, so we didn't even have our announcer. It was just the two of us, duking it out.

After a while, we dropped our gloves and boxed bare-knuckled.

Boxing without gloves hurts, maybe even more the day after. I'm not sure either of us really enjoyed it, but neither Coy nor I wanted to be the one to say no. We didn't want to appear weak or scared.

When we boxed with gloves, we always swung for the fences. We'd often take chances with huge, exaggerated hooks to the head. But boxing bare-knuckled, you have to be more calculated than that or you'll open yourself up to be hit. And getting hit hurts. Unlike the muffled blow of a boxing glove, a solid bare-knuckle strike to the face reverberates inside your head. First you feel the sharp pain of the knuckle contacting your cheek; then you hear the sound— a loud crack. So we did our best to protect our heads using an old-school boxing-style stance, body curled up with fists right in front of our faces.

When it was bare-knuckle time, Coy and I always fought in the middle of the courtyard. There were no lights illuminating your opponent, only the moonlight, which was usually just enough for me to make out his silhouette. I'd see him moving back and forth, and then without warning there'd be a fist flying at my face.

Coy was crafty and was often able to slip in punches to my head. But with that I'd move in closer. I'd always heard that if you hit a man hard in the body, his head will come down. So I'd aim for his ribs, cracking his face as his head lowered with each punch.

Those rounds never lasted as long. And I'm not sure if anyone ever really won. We just fought until we'd collapse onto the sand in two piles, heaving to catch our breath.

That was when the pain started to really bubble to the surface. I could feel the bruises forming, the throbbing growing louder. It may sound juvenile, but those battle wounds, the feeling that both of us had just endured something, it somehow made me feel more alive. And it sealed my brotherhood with Coy.

"Thanks for watching my team while I was away," I said.

"No sweat. They're good dudes," said Coy. "That Simon, man, he's on it."

"Yeah, he is. They are all good."

"So, Doc, are you cool now? Is everything cool with you?"

Nah, it really wasn't. But I wasn't ready to talk either.

So as we lay there in the moonlight, bruised and bloodied, Coy opened up to me. He shared some things about his past, his ex-wife, things that were haunting him, things he'd never told anyone else before. And I appreciated what he was doing.

And after awhile I shared some too. I talked about my struggles at work, the ambush, and about some personal things I'd been burying—memories that I had long ago drowned in beer and locked away deep inside my brain.

Sharing like that made me feel better. And I know it made Coy feel better too.

And I had to laugh. Samaritan's Purse could've saved a whole bunch of money on that Christian counselor—all they really needed to do was buy me and Coy a jar of seeco.

FOURTEEN

To: Fil Anderson

Sent: Saturday, May 14, 2005, 3:14:23 a.m.

Subject: Hey, man!

Howdy Fil,

It's great to hear from you my brotha. I am surprised at
the knowledge and the heart that your boy has for the
matters of this world. When I was in 9th grade the most
important thing on my mind was fitting in with the right
crowd. My biggest hurt in my heart was not getting the

girl. And my anger and frustration were directed, for some unknown reason, at my parents who I thought "didn't understand me."

I am comforted in knowing there are teenagers out there who give a damn about what is going on in this crazy place that we call "the world." I wish I could e-mail you an encouraging letter about our efforts here in Darfur. I wish I could say that things are changing, that the people are starting to return home, and that the government soldiers and the government-backed militias have stopped raping women and girls on a regular basis in the IDP camps that the majority of people in Darfur now call home.

However, I can't say these things. My heart has taken a beating these past 9 months because I can see what little effect our labors have had. Yes, we have been able to keep these people "alive" by giving them the basic needs of food and water. But what exactly does that mean? We have kept mothers and fathers alive so they can hear the news of their daughters' rapes. We have kept children alive so they can be crammed in an IDP camp, where each day that passes is another day stolen from their ever-fleeting childhood. Children quickly lose all sense of what it means to be young. They trade in their soccer ball for a bucket, and instead of walking to school every day, they are walking four and five hours to retrieve water.

So, in the end, have we really saved these people's lives?

What is the definition of *life*?

Is it eating, sleeping, breathing?

Or is it something much greater?

I don't have any answers. All I am left with when I lie down on my cot at night to try and catch some sleep are questions. I feel sick because sometimes I think the people in Rwanda had it easier than the people in Darfur. The mass extinction of that group of people was carried out over a handful of months. However these people's deaths are being drawn out daily, all the while the news of rapes and deaths of family members are funneled into their ears.

Fil, my man, I am glad that the Lord has been tugging on your heart. These people need all the prayers and help that they can get. I'll be looking forward to getting back and taking you out on that lunch date that we were supposed to go on a little over a year ago. And tell that boy of yours that whatever road he's on in his life, it sure seems to be the right one to me. I wish I had taken that road when I was in 9th grade instead of the one that I ended up taking.

Hey, If you haven't gotten any of the other group e-mails that I have sent out, you can e-mail my dad and I'm sure he will send you some more, or all, if you want them. I must say though . . . they ain't all pretty.

Well, bro, you take care of yourself.

Much Love,

Doc

. . .

If I told you that I came back from Kenya all raring to go, ready to save the world again—it'd be a lie. I hate to admit it, but the ambush took a lot out of me. That's not exactly the way I thought getting shot at would affect me. But it messed with me. Hard.

Deep down I knew I needed to get back to the field, back to water work, but I also wondered how productive I could actually be in this state of mind. Truthfully—and I'm embarrassed to say this—I had become so frustrated with Darfur and the politics of aid work and the frickin' Janjaweed that I was over it.

I wasn't sure anymore that I could be of much help to these people who needed it so badly. But saying that last sentence aloud made me sick to my stomach. *Screw that. I'm not a quitter.*

I still had a little over three months left on my contract, and I refused to fly away from Darfur without leaving the place at least a little better than I'd found it.

Easier said than done.

In one way or another, the Janjaweed had seemingly done their best to destroy every single water project I'd attempted in Darfur. And when I realized those soldiers who were shooting at me and my team in Teige were likely the very same guys who had raped the young girls of Leiba, I was livid (again).

Maybe the counselor in Kenya wasn't full of crap after

all. This wasn't just about the shooting, was it? It was the undercurrents. The reason for the fighting. The reason those SLA troops went to Teige to confront the Janjaweed in the first place.

Years ago, a girl I was in love with was raped while we were dating. We both knew the man who did it. And I still kick myself for not being there that night when she needed me most. But how could I have known?

It all came flooding back: driving her to the hospital, waiting three hours for her to be seen, the fluorescent lights in the emergency room flickering like mad, the doctor pulling back the gown to reveal her bruised and battered legs. I could clearly see the marks he'd left from using his elbows to force her thighs apart.

Suddenly my brain started doing what brains do best: filing, cataloging memories, comparing them to others. That feeling of rage, the uncontrollable desire to find her rapist—and kill him—felt a little bit like the feelings that bubbled up whenever I saw a GoS soldier or the Janjaweed.

Unearthing the rape connection didn't solve any problems, but it did, somehow, give me the drive I needed to continue in Darfur.

The next step was to get back up to Jebel Marra—so I could finish what I had started. The bucket-chlorination program we'd established in that area lacked one final, critical component: the two hundred thousand chlorine tablets that were in the back of the Buffalo when we got ambushed.

Of course, driving a convoy up to Feina again wasn't an option anymore, but David Del Conte was able to line us up with a UN helicopter airlift.

The huge white Russian-built transport helicopter was operated by the UN's World Food Programme, and was headed on its weekly flight to drop personnel and supplies in far western Darfur. As the old helicopter rattled and clunked its way through the air, I had to laugh. Just like the AK-47s and Antonov bombers, it seemed that all things Russian-made were clunky and loud, but also somehow always durable enough to be operable far beyond what one would consider a typical life span for this type of equipment.

As the helicopter made a wide clockwise orbit around the village of Feina, I could see the villagers, especially the children, running out of their mud huts, eager to see who was landing in their village. They no doubt saw the occasional flyover, but helicopters almost never landed there.

The pilot slowly crabbed his way over to a wide-open spot just to the east of the village near the main road. By the time we touched down there were hundreds of villagers standing there, waving, their jellabiyas whipping wildly in the rotor wash.

"Okay, Doc, I'll be back for you guys in one week!" the pilot shouted to me over the thwacking of the blades.

"Sounds good!"

"Same spot," he said, "same time next week!"

I gave the pilot the thumbs-up and he was gone.

The sultan was among those gathered to greet our helicopter. He shook my hand heartily, then pulled me in for a hug. And he seemed especially pleased when he saw Amir and Hilary heaving the boxes of chlorine tabs from the landing zone.

We dropped the bulk of our load with the sultan for his men to distribute among Feina's residents and the nearby villages. The rest we planned to carry to Saboon El Fagor, a remote village way up in the mountains, so the sultan loaned us a pair of his donkeys to pack the load.

My team and I hiked for six hours straight, some seventeen miles—much of it uphill, on rough, rock-strewn paths. Once we reached Saboon El Fagor we delivered the rest of our chlorine tablet supply and spent the afternoon teaching the villagers about proper sanitation and how to implement the bucket-chlorination program.

With four days left before our helicopter was to return for us in Nyala, we decided to use the remaining days to continue up the mountain, visiting with several even more remote villages and doing water assessments.

I also planned to take a side trip to see the Deriba Caldera, a dormant volcano perched at the highest point of the Jebel Marra mountains at an elevation of 9,980 feet. Inside the mouth of this massive crater, some three miles in diameter and fifteen hundred feet deep, there is a pair of lakes, one of which is said to be haunted. Pretty much from the beginning of my time on the ground in Darfur, I'd heard people (both locals and fellow aid workers alike) talk about this lake and some kind of evil creature that supposedly lurks beneath, coming to the surface only to snatch and kill livestock, locals, even a curious aid worker, as one story goes. It's Darfur's answer to Loch Ness and its famous monster, Nessie.

Now, I've never been one to believe in superstitions, so I was dead set on hiking down into the crater and swimming in that fricking "haunted lake." And you can be sure, at the next aid worker cocktail party held at David's compound, I'd be sporting my adventurous tale like a brand-new Harley tattoo.

We got an early start, leaving Saboon El Fagor around six-thirty a.m. We rented a couple horses and hired a local guide who would lead us to the other villages and, eventually, help us pick our way up the circuitous path to the crater.

Along the trail we encountered slender corridors of rain forest tucked away amid the desert, usually where a spring or small creek trickled down the hill. In these verdant nooks of green, I spotted the most animal life I'd ever seen in Darfur, including rowdy monkeys and many unique birds, such as a huge brownish red–and–black bird that looked much like a bald eagle, only larger. We also ran across the occasional wild pig. Naturally Muslims don't eat pigs, but had I been by myself I would have tried to snatch one of those creatures up and roasted it right there on the mountain. Man, I missed my good ol' North Carolina barbecue.

We visited a few more small mud-hut villages. For the most part, all of the villages we encountered looked similar to

Feina, but they became much smaller and less well equipped the farther up the mountain we traveled. And many of these villagers had never seen a white person, so it was always entertaining to watch their faces as I ambled up the trail.

At each village we spent time surveying the water, sanitation, and hygiene needs of the community. Although these people had many of the same basic needs—access to clean water and education—as their fellow countrymen down in the desert, in many ways these villagers seemed to have much more sustainable lives. That gave me a little hope.

The starkest difference between these little mountain villages and the others we'd visited in the region was the children. In pretty much every other Darfuri village, the children seemed to have an air of uncertainty about them. Sure, they were still kids, and they would jump at the chance to play whenever possible, even if that meant kicking around a ball of trash or beating a homemade drum. But there was always a small black cloud of worry following them around. In the back of their mind they would be worried about when their dad or uncle or brother would leave to join the rebel forces; they worried about walking outside their villages at night for fear they'd be raped; and they worried that the sound of thunder they heard at night wasn't a bad storm, but rather the sound of so many Janjaweed galloping toward them in the darkness or an Antonov bomber dispatched by the Sudanese government to unleash living hell onto their village. These were the same worries that drove many villagers to retreat nightly to nearby caves, where they could be safe from their enemies. What kind of a life is that for a kid?

Fortunately, the higher the elevation and the farther from the Janjaweed's reach we trekked, the more at ease the children seemed. More innocent. Happier. Seeing children living like children are supposed to really buoyed my spirits.

Continuing up the mountain, we had sweeping views of fresh, fertile green valleys as well as harsh moonscapes of nothing but sharp, volcanic rock. In spots we were riding along narrow paths on the edge of two-thousand-foot cliffs. The sound of my horse's hooves slipping on the loose rock and scree really got my adrenaline pumping—and I loved every minute of it.

Around noon, Amir abruptly stopped his donkey on a knife-edge ridge. He dismounted, turned to face Mecca, rolled his prayer mat out on the rocky ground, and began his daily salah, just as he'd done five times a day, every day since I'd met him. Now, I haven't done the exact math, but I figured that over the past six months I'd witnessed Amir, Ismael, and my other Muslim workers praying nearly a thousand times. While I respected their tradition, I rarely paid much attention to their prayer times.

But after the ambush I often caught myself watching their salahs more closely. As Amir moved quietly through his typical chanting, standing, kneeling, and bowing with the expansive Jebel Marra valley soaring below, I felt like we all had something real to be thankful for that day. So I said a prayer myself, something I had been doing a lot more of in recent weeks.

Just before sunset, we reached the rim of the Deriba Caldera. Deep below I could see one lake clearly. It's known as the "female lake" to locals and, incidentally, has an even higher salt content than the Dead Sea. The other one, the haunted "male lake," lay out of sight, deeper within the mouth of the volcano, protected on all sides by steep rock walls.

As I steered my horse toward the path that led down into the crater, the others stopped abruptly, my guide mumbling something in Arabic.

"He says, 'I'm not going to that lake. There's an evil thing that lives there that'll suck you in,'" Hilary said, translating for the guide. "Amir and I will stay here. He says you shouldn't go either."

"Come on, guys; just go down there with me. I'm gonna swim."

"No, thank you, Mr. Doc. We stay here."

It felt as though I was riding my horse down into some huge crater on the moon. It was barren and eerily quiet. As I neared the male lake, I had to dismount and walk my horse down the steep trail. I could see a dark purple-and-black cloud gathering near the rim of the crater above. I could tell a storm was on the way, but I was too close to the lake now to turn back.

By the time I reached the deep emerald lake, the wind was whipping wildly, with occasional lightning cracks nearby.

I tied my horse to some nearby brush and walked to the water's edge. The water was surprisingly clear. I found a large volcanic rock nearby and sat to pull off my boots. Walking gingerly across the sharp volcanic rock and into the water, I noticed that the lake had a two-foot-wide shelf of rock that suddenly gave way to black nothingness, unbelievably deep.

Do you really wanna swim in there? I asked myself.

Before I could answer, I was interrupted by deep guttural barking. The sound was loud and coming from all around me. I looked up and saw a bunch of baboons hanging in a stand of sparse trees nearby. I wasn't sure what their barking meant, but it sounded a lot like laughter. They were mocking me.

I knelt down slowly, cupped the water, and splashed it onto my face. I expected to feel refreshed, but as soon as the water touched my skin, all I felt was this sense of urgency deep within my gut. Something inside me was saying, *Get back on your horse and ride the hell out of here.*

My heart was pumping like wild.

You can't come this far and not at least go for a quick swim, said one side of my brain. *What are you scared of?*

Truthfully I'm still not sure what I was scared of, but the other side of my brain, the part that was in control of my feet, wouldn't let me take a single step deeper into that lake. I decided I'd rather admit to the others that I hadn't been man enough to swim in the lake than take my chances in that eerie water.

As I mounted my horse and rode away from the lake, the

baboons barked and howled even more loudly than before. They were definitely mocking me now.

By the time I returned to the crater's rim, my team was ready to roll. The sun had already set, and the storm pretty much had the top of the mountain socked in. Everybody was soaking wet, and the temperature had dropped quickly, so we rode as fast as we could toward a small mud hut perched on a nearby ridge that we'd seen on the way up.

There were two men hunkered down inside, and they warmly invited us all to join them. We shared steaming cups of chai tea. Hilary did most of the talking, but the men wouldn't stop staring at me. It was clear they might have never before seen someone with white skin.

"So what is this thing that lives in the lake?" I asked the older man, who looked to be at least fifty, with a scraggly gray beard and a dirty yellowed jellabiya.

"'I saw the animal of the lake that sucks things into the water many years ago, when I was a young boy,'" translated Hilary. "'It was very large. Longer than two men In length, with huge, long jaws.'"

With that the old man snapped his arms together over and over, pantomiming the chomping, just like a child pretending to be a crocodile.

That got me thinking. This evil monster of the lake may have simply been a large crocodile, or even a family of them. It made perfect sense, and would easily explain the locals' stories of grazing livestock that regularly disappeared near the edge of that freshwater lake. It also explained the uneasy feeling I felt in my gut. And I was glad that for once I had actually listened to my more cautious side rather than always flying by the seat of my pants.

The next morning, we began heading back down the mountain to Feina, covering some fifty miles of trail in all. Spending extended time out in the field like that, far from the things that had been weighing on my mind, felt good. I was beginning to relax again.

And seeing Amir and the others stop to do their daily prayers, even as we hiked, served as inspiration. I started reading the Bible, the one that I always carried around with me in my pack, with a newfound fervor. I did most of my reading by flashlight at night after my team had all fallen asleep.

I grew up reading the Bible—it's pretty much unavoidable when your dad is a preacher man—but when I was a kid, reading the Bible was always something we were required to do. This time, reading the book again smack in the middle of one of the most beautiful mountain ranges I'd ever seen, I began taking something different away from the Bible.

I loved reading about how Jesus hung out with drunks and hookers, and that his first miracle, as I could best calculate, was making approximately a hundred and twenty gallons of wine so that a wedding party could continue rocking out instead of ending early because there was no more booze. And I was fired up when I began to learn the uncensored versions of those Bible stories that I had heard as a child, like when David, after knocking Goliath out, took the giant's sword, cut off his head, and proceeded to carry it around for the rest of the day, wielding it as a trophy.

Instead of making me feel like I was being preached at or judged, the stories spoke to me. And what I read made me feel hopeful. It encouraged me that I didn't have to be a perfect do-gooder to actually do something good in this world.

It also made me yearn for the opportunity to one day become a husband and a father. I can't explain why exactly. Maybe it was Ismael hounding me about why I wasn't married yet, or seeing Amir playing lovingly with his children. Or maybe all that desert living just finally gave me some clarity, telling me it was time to grow up. Whatever it was, that last night in Jebel Marra, I prayed out loud to God, asking him to spare my life and to get me out of that crazy place so I could one day experience firsthand the love of being a husband and a father. What I didn't bargain for was the fact that from that day on, I was for the first time legitimately scared whenever I went back into the field. Before, I was younger and reckless. Suddenly, I guess, I had a real reason to stay alive.

FIFTEEN

W e started digging early that morning. It was July, so we knew it was going to get really hot, really quick—daytime temperatures in Darfur that time of the year can easily reach a hundred and thirty degrees Fahrenheit. Plus, there was much more to do. The digging was only the beginning.

There were at least a dozen of us men working together in a wide-open spot on the western edge of Nyala, just past the outskirts of town. Very little vegetation grew there—the place was all sand and rocks. In fact, many local women collected the smallest of these rocks, arranged them in piles on the roadside according to size, and sold them as gravel. I always made a point of buying my gravel from these women for whatever building projects we had.

We each took turns digging; the first foot or so was mostly loose sand, but that soon gave way to a thick crust. Slowly we chipped away at the hard earth until our hole was approximately three feet deep and about two and a half feet wide and seven feet long. That was when Amir jumped down inside the hole.

He stood at one end, then quickly dragged his left foot lengthwise along the dirt, leaving a dusty path about a foot wide and six feet long. Without a word, an older man handed him the shovel. Amir began digging again, quickly yet carefully, within the outline he had created. All of the men took turns digging the smaller hole.

I was struck by their precision and efficiency. It was as if this digging was instinctual.

Once the second hole-within-a-hole was neatly carved out to a depth of three feet, all of the men from Ismael's family and I then walked over to the open bed of a small, dusty white pickup truck and lifted out Ismael's limp body. He had been dead just over twelve hours and was wrapped in a white linen shroud customary for Muslim burials.

As we gently lowered Ismael's body down to Amir, who was standing in the hole, thoughts and emotions were storming inside me. I was heartbroken for Ismael's family. I was pissed at the Janjaweed for wrecking everything they touched. Most of all, I felt like Ismael's death was ultimately my fault. I believed he was probably murdered because of his work with me, bringing fresh water to the very people the Janjaweed were mandated to kill.

For the past three weeks, my team had been working extra hard. We rehabbed a dozen old wells, completed chlorine tablet drops to rural villages, and dug hundreds of latrines for Sania Afandu, as well as establishing a new hygiene-education program. We had been very busy, and I was proud of my guys, so I gave them a couple days off to rest.

Ismael hopped on the bus to spend the weekend in his home village visiting with his wife and three children and bringing them his week's wages. On the half-day ride back to Nyala and back to work, Ismael's bus was stopped just after nightfall about one mile short of the Nyala police checkpoint. Four Janjaweed soldiers blocked the bus, aiming AK-47s at the windshield, while two others pushed open the door and climbed aboard.

One by one the men forced all of the passengers out the door. They lined them all up, men, women, and children, and made them lie facedown in the sand. A soldier walked back and forth along the line of frightened travelers, interrogating them about their involvement with the SLA. Then he picked out four men, including Ismael, and loaded the rest of the people back onto the bus.

With all of the passengers watching, the soldiers forced Ismael and the others onto their knees, yanking their hands behind their backs. Then they lowered their rifles and shot each one of them in the back of the head, execution style. It all happened very quickly.

Amir gently rolled his friend onto his right side, facing Mecca, and slipped him into the smaller interior hole. Ismael fit perfectly inside. Amir carefully covered the hole with large, flat, chalky white stones and climbed out. Following Ismael's father's lead, we each took turns shoveling dirt atop the stones, slowly refilling the grave.

Everyone wanted to pitch in. I think maybe in a strange way it helped with the healing process of losing a son, father, and friend. Of course, in the Muslim culture, burials are an event that only the men are allowed to attend; the rest of the family would feast together night and day for the next three days in celebration of Ismael's life.

From that whole event, the one thing that was seared into my memory, the thing I still ponder most during those dark times when I have neither strength nor will to suppress such thoughts, is the image of Amir dragging his foot across the bottom of the grave without hesitation to perfectly fit our friend into his final resting place.

I lived in Darfur from August 2004 to August 2005. During that year, the UN estimated that more than a hundred and twenty thousand people were killed as part of the fighting between the SLA and the Janjaweed and, of course, the genocide of the black African population. Death was all around me during my tenure. Hell, I even came close to dying a few times myself. But it took seeing Amir measure out a man-width hole using the length of his foot for me to realize that, sadly, the Darfuri people had become experts in the matters of death. I think whatever scraps of innocence I had left in my body were buried with Ismael that day in the grave I helped dig.

From: Doc Hendley
To: Jeff Hendley
Sent: Saturday, July 2, 2005, 4:45:23 p.m.
Subject: What I learned today

Supposedly we learn something new everyday. Today, I learned how to dig a grave. I lost one of my men last night. His name was Ismael. I gave my guys a couple days off, so Ismael went to see his children in a town just south of Nyala. He was returning to Nyala last night on a small bus. When he was within 1 mile of the Nyala police checkpoint, 6 men ambushed his truck. The driver stopped and everyone was forced out of the bus and put on the ground face down. Ismael and 3 others were shot in the back and killed.

I hoped my last six weeks would be easier. I hoped I could get out of here without much more drama. Looks like things don't always work out like we hope.

Happy 4th, everyone. Celebrate our great country
a little extra for me!!! I love all y'all and hope to see
you soon.

Doc

If I'm being totally honest, I had hoped to cruise through
my final weeks in Darfur. I was just counting down the days
before I could hop aboard a Midair Collision flight and get
the hell out of that desert. But losing Ismael really made me
reevaluate my remaining time on the job.

Sure, maybe I risked my neck a little more than most aid
workers by striving to bring clean water to those living in the
UN no-go zones. But in the end all those hand pumps we
fixed were bound to break down again. And the Janjaweed
would continue doing their damnedest to destroy everything
we had worked to accomplish.

So what's the point? I asked myself. *What have I truly
accomplished here?*

Looking for an answer, I kept coming back to my men,
my team of hardworking Darfuris, like Amir, Hilary, Ismael,
and Simon. I had developed a deep respect and affection for
those guys. It's funny; if someone would've told me a year
earlier that I'd soon be great friends with a group of East
African men, I would've had a hard time comprehending
the thought. And beyond that, in spite of our obvious differ-

ences, I became very close with all of my Sudanese brothers. I trusted them with my life, and they trusted me. We had become kindred spirits.

And in some ways, my time in Darfur reminded me of my years working as a bartender. I never was the fastest pour in Raleigh or an expert at mixing those froofy cocktails and shots. But I was very successful because I connected with people and developed relationships with my customers.

In the same vein, I definitely wasn't the model aid worker either. Hell, when I first got into this I didn't know the first thing about digging wells or fixing hand pumps, just like I didn't know how to mix drinks when I was hired at Club Mojo. But I went with it. And I connected with people, my men, fellow aid workers, the refugees, even the gnarliest, most hardened SLA rebels. I also eventually figured out which "patrons" to pay the most attention to, like the sultans, sheikhs, and SLA commanders, not the rowdy drunks at the end of the bar screaming for more shots.

That got me thinking: If my greatest successes revolved around the people, then the best way to really make a lasting difference in Darfur had nothing to do with fixing the most wells in the shortest period of time. It had to do with the people.

I realized that what I needed to do was to empower the locals, to give them the tools they needed to solve their own problems and become self-sufficient.

Although I had only five weeks left in Darfur, my team

and I rallied to create a program to train villagers how to fix their own wells. We put together hand-pump repair kits with tools and supplies, and quickly began returning to the villages where we had already rehabilitated hand pumps or dug new wells. In each village, we established two- and three-person repair teams (we called them water leaders), teaching them everything they needed to know to keep their own wells in good working order. We also gathered the parents in each village, instructing them on proper hygiene and sanitation skills for their families, because poor hygiene can sicken as many children as dirty water.

Though a lot of work remained undone by the time my contract ended, things were definitely headed in the right direction. My men knew the mission and were doing a great job reaching as many villages as possible. Meanwhile, Coy stepped up to fill my role and manage the water team. I felt relieved that I would be leaving my group in my friend's capable hands.

I quietly left Nyala late one afternoon. There was no big fanfare. No tearful good-byes. I simply boarded a plane bound for Khartoum with nothing but my now faded blue Kelty backpack and the satisfaction that I had finally been able to put a plan into motion that would hopefully make a lasting difference.

Before leaving Sudan for good, I stopped in at an orphanage in Khartoum. Five months earlier, around Christmastime, during a quick trip to the capital, I met an amazing woman named Miriam. She too was from the States, and just a few years earlier sold everything she owned and moved to Khartoum to open an orphanage in one of the city's worst slums. She funded the orphanage entirely using her own money, and although she was successfully housing, feeding, and educating more than a dozen street kids—many of whom had been addicted to sniffing glue—her orphanage was in dire need of help.

They had no running water. Instead they were getting all their water for drinking and cooking from a big barrel that was filled by runoff from the street. Naturally, the children were perpetually sick with diarrhea and other stomach ailments.

During my time in Sudan, I was constantly searching for worthwhile water projects on which to use the Wine to Water funds we'd raised back in the States. While we had supported dozens of projects in Darfur in conjunction with Samaritan's Purse, as soon as I stepped inside Miriam's orphanage I knew I'd found the perfect recipient for our first project fully funded by Wine to Water.

We installed a two-thousand-liter tank and gravity-fed water system that provided the orphanage with clean running water for drinking, showering, toilets, and washing clothes. It may not have been the fanciest water system, but it worked. And seeing the grinning faces of those children, who were obviously healthier—and happier—than ever, let me know we'd had a real impact on their lives.

Although the slums of Khartoum were not a pleasant place, it was definitely worlds away from the fighting going on in Darfur, so I knew that our water system would be there to stay, bringing clean water to these children for many years to come. At least this was one project that the Janjaweed wouldn't be able to screw up.

SIXTEEN

By mid-August, I was back living in North Carolina—
but was far from settled. Thanks to the rough reentry
during my R & R in January, my family was prepared
for my return. They knew I needed a little space and time to get
acclimated to life back in the States—and they gave it to me.

But the culture shock seemed heavier this time, probably
because I didn't know how long I was going to feel this way.
On R & Rs in the past, at least I had the comfort of knowing I had to endure only a week or so, and then I'd be back in
Darfur. I guess this time the unknown just scared the crap out
of me.

Although moving to Raleigh would have been the quick-
est, easiest way for me to get back into the swing of things

and get a job (because of my strong contacts there), I also knew it'd be way too easy for me to fall right back into the wild life that awaited me in the bars along Glenwood Avenue.

So I moved in with my parents in Boone.

Unfortunately, the job prospects in that quiet little mountain town were nonexistent, but something about the place—the cool mountain air and my afternoon Harley rides on those lazy two-lane roads—promised the calm I so badly needed.

Ironically, those gentle green mountains and my quiet life there also became the source of a lot of guilt. Boone is quite literally the diametrical opposite of Darfur, in both landscape and lifestyle. And because of that I soon developed strong feelings of shame for having such luck in life while so many people were still suffering in the deserts of Darfur.

I had seen so many horrors over the past year, and those memories were tough to shake. I had nightmares almost every night after returning home. And there was one recurring dream that especially haunted me.

I'd always be walking on the street in Nyala near the compound, on my way to go out to eat or to an OCHA meeting. Then suddenly, at the end of the street, a truck full of Janjaweed would appear. I would sprint as hard as I could through town, but the soldiers always seemed to corner me in an area near the Nyala trash dump. I'd be stuck, and then this Janjaweed guy with a scraggly black beard and an AK-47 would walk right up and shoot me in the head. The sound was deafening, with a blinding blast. The pain was immense.

Then I'd wake up sweating, totally disoriented, thinking I was in my bed at the compound in Nyala.

During my waking hours I was preoccupied with figuring out what I should be doing with my life. I knew I wanted to continue growing Wine to Water, but it was never something I thought of as a potential career. Instead, Wine to Water was always just something I wanted to do on the side, because I felt good about it and I loved it.

Still, I needed a job.

With a huge earthquake having devastated Pakistan, and the Hurricane Katrina floods ravaging New Orleans, there was plenty of aid work to be done, and I considered signing another contract with Samaritan's Purse. But Kenny Isaacs wasn't working there anymore, and I didn't get the warm reception I once had. In the end, I knew as well as they did that I probably wasn't the best fit to continue with their organization.

I also considered a bunch of other options, including working as a policeman in Charlotte, opening my own Harley shop in Boone, even going back to school for a master's degree in environmental science. But nothing quite fit, so I eventually did some bartending again and landed gigs playing guitar and singing in bars and restaurants around Boone.

One night, not long after moving back to Boone, I rode my Harley over to a popular bar called the Library. While I wasn't yet back to normal and looking to meet new people, I was in need of cold beer and to listen to some live rock and roll. So I posted up in the corner of the bar, as far away from people as possible, and just sang along into my beer bottle.

Around the time I was belting out my own rendition of Lynyrd Skynyrd's "Freebird," I looked up and was suddenly face-to-face with a beautiful young blond woman with big brown eyes. Her name was Amber Waters, and as soon as her last name left her full red lips, I should've known it was meant to be.

"Your real name is Doc?" she said, holding out her hand demurely for a shake.

"Yes . . . well, no . . . my real name is Dickson," I stammered, "but everyone calls me Doc."

"Ah, Dickson. I like that better," she said with a sweet little grin. "I will call you that."

I took Amber for a ride on my Harley the very next afternoon. We hit it off immediately, and like a fairy tale or some Nicholas Sparks romance novel, our love blossomed quickly and fully.

There was just something different about Amber. In front of other people, she was lighthearted and fun and sometimes put on the cute ditzy-blond act; but one on one, I realized she was actually very deep and intelligent. Amber possessed a compassion for people, similar in intensity to mine, but different. She spent much of her free time working with special-needs youth and volunteering in nursing homes, and eventually took a job teaching special education to adults at the local community college. And she always put the needs of others before her own, almost to a fault.

Amber turned out to be exactly what I needed to pull myself together after coming back from Darfur. She never once pressured me to talk about my time in the desert, or even my wilder times before that. However, Amber was always there to listen to me when I needed to get something out, and supported me whenever I needed encouragement. On the other hand, she never had any problem calling me out whenever I was off base. I really respected her for that.

By January, after only six months dating Amber, I knew there was no other woman in the world I wanted to spend my life with and have as the mother of my children. So I asked Amber to marry me.

To this day, if anyone asks me the scariest moment of my life, hands down I would say it was the night I proposed. Never before had I invested so much of myself in someone. And the thought that all of that could be gone with a simple *no* scared me silly. Thank God she said yes.

From: Doc Hendley
To: WTW mailing list
Sent: Friday, June 2, 2006, 9:34 p.m.
Subject: Wine to Water stuff in the fall

Howdy all y'all,

It's been a long while since I've written, so let me give everyone a quick update on what's been going on. I'll try and give y'all the short version. I got back in August, and not too long after I met a young lady named Amber. I was going to go back to work with Samaritan's Purse, but I would have been right back in Africa and I wasn't quite ready to leave my new lady friend. So in February Amber's stepfather, Daniel, offered me a job with his insurance company so that I could continue living in Boone.

Anyway . . . not too long after I got the job I asked Amber to marry me. . . . (As a side note I proposed under the disco ball at Skate World with my speed skates on. It was romantic in a way that only few can appreciate!) So, Amber and I are getting hitched this summer here in Boone. I've been pretty busy the past few months starting a new job, planning a wedding, building a house, and more.

So, that is why not many of y'all have heard much from me. Now . . . back to Wine to Water. I'm sure all y'all know what a huge impact everyone was able to have in the lives of the folks we helped in Sudan. This fall, we are planning to broaden our efforts in Darfur. I am trying to get speaking engagements in different universities in North and South Carolina to raise awareness for the Darfur region and to educate people on what is really going on in the area.

I don't have bullets whizzing by my head at the moment but I could still use everyone's prayers— obviously for my upcoming marriage and new job, but also for Wine to Water. My new job will allow me the freedom to continue running Wine to Water from here in Boone, but in the near future we will probably be looking for someone to formally take over and manage what I am unable to manage. My dad and I have been volunteering our own time to do everything up until now, and we plan on continuing to do so. But, if we continue to grow like we did last year, we will soon need someone in a more permanent managing position.

Thank y'all so much for your support. I will hopefully be in contact with everyone soon in order to give a better picture of what things are going to look like for WTW in the fall.

Much love,
Doc

. . .

Amber and I were married in July, and I had already started working for her stepfather, Daniel, at his insurance business in Boone. Though it was a good job, no matter how hard I tried to convince myself, my heart was just not in insurance.

I had trouble focusing, and the only time I got excited at the office was when an e-mail would come through from Darfur from Simon, Coy, or Andy, or when I'd read the news online at CNN or the BBC describing political unrest and natural disasters around the world. All I could think of was how I'd love to be there in the field doing something to help instead of sitting there behind a desk. But my commitment was to Daniel, so I put my head down and continued to plug away at my insurance job.

The most frustrating thing was that even though I had full intentions of continuing to build my organization, between my full-time job plus my evening gigs singing in bars, it seemed like I was never able to find enough time to devote to Wine to Water.

Then, one day at work in September, I had been e-mailing back and forth with Coy, who was still in Darfur. We were discussing Wine to Water—where I saw it going and how I planned on getting it there. Coy's contract with Samaritan's Purse was due to be up in a couple of months, and he volunteered to help me get Wine to Water going during the six months he had off before he had to leave on his next contract. The prospect of working with Coy to build my organization got my heart pumping. I hadn't been that energized since I was in Darfur working in the field. I couldn't wait for Coy to get back to the States so we could get started. Then the phone rang. A man wanted an insurance quote, and the harsh reality of where my life was headed sank in— *I'm an insurance salesman now.*

I was totally defeated.

Later that night, when Amber came home from work, she could tell immediately something was wrong. I started to explain what I was upset about, but she already knew.

"Look!" she said firmly. "I understand why you are working with my stepdad selling insurance and why you still play music. I know that you are just trying to provide for me, because apparently that's what a husband is supposed to do. But you need to know something—I didn't marry an insurance salesman. I didn't marry a bartender or a bar singer. I married the man I met at the Library who had the weight of the world on his shoulders and was trying everything he could to fix its problems."

As she spoke my heart beat wildly, and snapshots of Darfur raced through my brain. I didn't know how to respond.

"I have a good job with enough pay to cover the bills. And I want you to know that being a good husband to me isn't about providing money. It's about being the man you're meant to be. If you stop everything else you're doing to pursue Wine to Water, I will be behind you every step of the way, encouraging you and believing in you, even if I have to work a full-time job the rest of my life."

Although working a desk job selling insurance and succumbing to the day-to-day grind of typical Western life wasn't me, I would do it all over again just to hear Amber say those words to me one more time. There are few feelings in this world greater than knowing that the person you love most believes in you and is your biggest fan.

It took a few months for me to transition out of the insurance business, but starting that very next morning I put our new plan into motion. Coy soon returned from Darfur and, in early February, on my first day full-time with Wine to Water, we set out to find office space.

The first place we looked at was a great space in downtown Boone just off the main street, but we couldn't afford it. Later that afternoon, by happenstance, I ran into the building's owner (what can I say; Boone is a small town). Pretty much as soon as I explained the mission of Wine to Water and our situation to the man, he immediately offered to give it to us for the first three months rent-free.

It must've been meant to be.

My dad donated a couple of old computers, desks, and a big ol' filing cabinet.

I remember sitting there that first afternoon in our new office, staring at the empty filing cabinet, wondering if it might actually be filled up one day.

SEVENTEEN

I t was great having Coy around to help me kick-start Wine to Water. Besides having him assist with all of the mundane tasks of setting up an office—just like I'd done back in Nyala a couple of years earlier—knowing that my buddy would be there every morning was a great motivating force.

It was also good having someone in town who understood exactly where I was coming from. Although Coy and I hung up our boxing gloves once back stateside, we did do our best to reunite (at least half of) our old Darfur band. Together we played gigs at the local bars under the unofficial name Second-rate Sexy, but we eventually changed it to Shebeen, an Irish word for an illegal drinking establishment.

Coy and I are very similar in personality. We're both personable, hardworking, and good public speakers, and we're dreamers. We spent a lot of time together in the office having spirited discussions about where Wine to Water could and should be headed. I had big aspirations for building the organization into an international nonprofit capable of bringing clean water to people all over the globe.

By that time we had raised around forty thousand dollars for Wine to Water, more than half of which was generated by those regular e-mail updates I wrote from Darfur. It didn't take long before those e-mails went viral, friends forwarding them from one friend to another, and soon I was getting e-mails (and donations) from lots of folks I'd never even met.

Through that grassroots e-mail network, I also learned about worthwhile water projects. I was approached by a friend of a friend of a friend about supporting a project for a leper colony on the outskirts of New Delhi, India. They had an old well, but it suddenly began producing only high-salinity water that was unfit for drinking. For a year they were without clean water. However, within just days of opening our new office, Coy and I were able to help fund and direct the building of a new running-water system for the colony. With a success like that right out of the gate we were energized, and Wine to Water developed some valuable momentum.

However, it turned out that Coy and I both shared another

personality trait—lack of attention to details and minutiae. While this usually made for an entertaining work atmosphere, the office had more of the air of a bachelor pad than an international aid organization. In fact, *organization* was the thing we were missing.

But that all changed one afternoon when a young blond woman came wandering into the Wine to Water office. Her name was Annie Clawson, and we expected her to be simply a curious local, like the other folks who had stopped by over the past weeks. As it turned out, though, Annie used to live in Bangkok, Thailand, where she was a schoolteacher, and most recently, she had worked for the Children's Heart Project medical ministry, where she handled the complicated logistics of bringing needy children from developing countries to the United States for heart surgeries. Annie told us that though her job was rewarding, the past few years had also been very trying at times, and she was looking forward to a break.

"So what are you doing now?" asked Coy.

"Well, I'm done with aid work; that's for sure," she said. "I was thinking of doing something totally different—maybe landscaping."

"Well, if you're interested, we're hiring," I said. "And you're hired, if you're interested."

Annie just stood there. Confused. She hadn't come in search of a job—just innocently stopped in to see what Wine to Water was all about.

"Well, just consider this our first date," said Coy with a grin. "If you wanna talk again, we'll be here."

"Wait a second," she said. "What's going on?"

"If you're going to go do fricking landscaping, you might as well help us," I said. "Look, we're here not knowing how to do this office work, and apparently you're a genius at it."

"Seriously, guys, I need a break, and I'm really burned out."

"That's perfect, because we are too," I countered.

"I don't know, guys. And I'd have to think really long and hard about it."

Annie left our office puzzled—I was pretty sure we'd scared her away.

But two weeks later, she returned.

"These are all the reasons you shouldn't hire me. And if you read this and you still want to hire me, then I'll come to work for you," she said, handing me a piece of paper with a handwritten list covering both sides.

Coy looked over my shoulder as I started reading through the long list of reasons that were meant to turn us off.

"You're perfect," I said. "You're hired."

Annie turned out to be just the kind of person Coy and I needed to keep us organized and on track with our mission. She added the perfect balance to Wine to Water.

Right off the bat, Annie helped plan our first Wine to Water event in Boone, at Bistro Roca, a nice restaurant just outside of town. It raised five thousand dollars and, possibly more important, the awareness of Wine to Water locally.

Soon more donations began trickling in, while Annie helped schedule Coy and me to do presentations at many organizations in the region—Rotary clubs, high schools, churches—whoever would sit and listen to us talk about the world's water crisis and Wine to Water's mission.

In the same way that I established local water leaders in Darfur before my contract was up, to help make the villages more self-sufficient and involved in solving their own water problems, Coy and I came up with the idea to create water and sanitation-training facilities throughout Uganda and Ethiopia in East Africa, where locals could learn how to access clean water and how to construct their own water filters and rain-catchment devices, all of which would be made locally, using locally sourced materials.

Coy and I flew to Africa for an initial assessment of the water needs in several regions of East Africa that we had targeted.

While in the field, we met with groups of refreshingly committed locals. In Ethiopia, we found a local organization that came up with an inventive man-powered well-drilling machine made from leftover Land Cruiser truck parts.

In Kampala, Uganda, we worked with a local organization who was keen to establish water filters and rainwater-containment programs.

On one hand, it felt really good to get back to Africa. On the other hand, I knew I still wasn't the save-the-world super-hero with a water filter in one hand and an orphaned baby in the other. And this time I was more cautious and, honestly, a little nervous. I wasn't used to feeling that way, and it made me feel a little bit weak. I guess having someone I needed and wanted to come home to made for a completely different experience in the field.

From: Amber Hendley
To: Doc Hendley
Sent: Sunday, July 1, 2007, 1:29 a.m.
Subject: RE: From Uganda

Hey baby,

Thank you for your e-mails, they are what makes me want to get up in the morning. When I get an e-mail or hear from you it motivates me to keep truckin'.

I know this doesn't help the situation, but I am having a really hard time with you being gone. I haven't been acting myself around anyone and all I can do is cry, especially at night. I hate sleeping in my bed without you, I hate sleeping anywhere without you. Tonight I am at your parents' house because I couldn't bear spending another night in that house alone. I feel like everything that has gone on the past few weeks has just hit like a ton of bricks. I am sooo lonely . . . the only person that can fix that is thousands of miles away.

I am so proud of you for all your hard work. I'm upset with myself because I feel like I have been having a pity party. I look back on what I have been writing and all I see are things about me. I'm sorry. I know it's not easy for you either.

I prayed tonight that God would open as many doors as possible for you to make a difference. But most of all I thanked him for the opportunity he has given WTW and the vision he has given you to make these amazing things happen that will change people's lives. I love knowing that you are fulfilling your passion, which is to help others any way possible. I thank God for instilling dedication, honesty, and faithfulness in you. Without those gifts, you would not be able to see your vision through.

Honey, I love you and I don't know what I would do without you. Hurry and come home to me!!!

From: Doc Hendley
To: Amber Hendley
Sent: Monday, July 2, 2007, 9:32 a.m.
Subject: RE: RE: From Uganda

I don't have long to write this morning, we are heading to the slums of Kampala in a few minutes, but I just had to hop on the computer to tell you that I love you.

Thank you for the e-mail, and for your honesty. It kills me to know that you hurt so much. I can't do this work without you. I need you with me . . . all the time. I need you with every decision. I can't work to the best of my ability without you, and I don't think WTW will make it to its potential without you by my side.

I love you,
Doc

Back in Boone, Coy and I outlined our plan, which we had narrowed down to working in northern Uganda and southern Sudan, and submitted it for grant proposals to organizations that typically fund projects like that.

We also expanded our efforts to Cambodia, hooking up with a local organization to drill several wells. Initially we used local contractors to drill the first few wells, but our ultimate goal was to find a way to fund a new drill rig so the locals could drill their own wells throughout the region at a greatly reduced price.

By July 2007, Coy's time was up, and he headed back to Darfur on another contract with Samaritan's Purse, and eventually ended up working in southern Sudan for the UN. I hated to see him go, but Coy grew up in the field, and his heart is in the field.

Annie and I kept rocking it out.

In 2007, we raised around a hundred thousand dollars, and then doubled it for 2008, with nearly two hundred thousand dollars in donations. Although we were making real progress, my sights were still set on Wine to Water reaching our first million dollars as quickly as possible. In an effort to keep our administrative costs down, both Annie and I refused to take our full salary, some months drawing no wages at all.

It's one thing to work for free as a single guy or girl, but when you're a married man with a family to support, that takes it to another level. And in May 2008, I found out first-hand, as Amber and I had our first son, Beattie Hendley. Besides being the best day of my life, becoming a father also changed my perspective on the world's water crisis. Watching children in Africa dying from dirty water is tough, but nothing produces empathy like having your own child and imagining him in the same situation. Suddenly I had new-found respect for the parents I met in Darfur who were fighting to provide for their children. For the first time I was able to more fully imagine myself in the shoes of a parent help-lessly unable to provide something as simple as water for his child. And the feeling was unbearable.

In August, we received huge news—and the biggest do-nation in Wine to Water history. Our grant proposal was accepted by a sizable organization based in the U.K., and we were awarded a two-hundred-and-forty-thousand-dollar grant, to be paid out over three years. I was ecstatic. Sud-denly my dream of Wine to Water being large enough to make a real difference in the world's water crisis seemed more within reach.

I immediately returned to Africa to work with our local partners and prepare them to implement our plan. In northern Uganda, we built two water and sanitation-training facilities and distributed more than five hundred bio-sand water filters throughout the region. Meanwhile, we also created a curriculum to teach locals about proper sanitation and how to collect and use rainwater.

I was in Kampala spending the afternoon at the headquarters of our local partners when I received a phone call that absolutely gutted me.

"Is everything okay? What's wrong, Amber?"

She paused a bit before answering. "The doctor looked at Beattie's skull X-ray and thinks he's going to need surgery. She says it could be serious and that we'll need to see a specialist as soon as possible."

"Surgery?! A specialist?! What kind of specialist?" I said, pacing back and forth on the dirt street.

"The doctor thinks Beattie has something called craniosynostosis. Basically she said he has no soft spot, and because of that his brain will have restricted growth, which could lead to developmental delays and deformities or even worse if it's not operated on soon."

My throat tightened. It was difficult to speak.

"Dickson, I just looked it up online and saw some pictures of other children with it, and pictures of the surgery. It looks horrible."

Amber paused but she wasn't crying. She never cries right in the middle of something bad. She's always strong in the thick of a problem and then she lets go when she doesn't feel the need to be strong anymore.

"They have to cut huge portions of the skull away, leaving the brain exposed, before they sew the skin back. All the children wear helmets, because if they hit their heads after surgery they could die. I'm really scared, Doc, and I need you here with me."

"I know, darlin'. I'm scared too," I said. "I'll come home now."

That was pretty much the bulk of the conversation. We said little else—I guess neither one of us really knew what to say. We both just felt something terrible gnawing inside our guts, something we'd never felt before.

I wasn't supposed to leave Uganda for another week, but I immediately left for the airport to try to find space on an evening flight out.

EIGHTEEN

B eattie was indeed suffering from a congenital birth defect called craniosynostosis. Basically the soft spot on his head had closed prematurely, which resulted in insufficient room for his brain to grow properly. Without immediate surgery, the doctors warned that he might experience increased intracranial pressure, which could result in dangerous seizures, deformity, and developmental delays.

Amber quit her job immediately to be with Beattie fulltime as we struggled through this. And though I continued with Wine to Water, I was a total mess. I had trouble focusing on anything, and was easily agitated—I'm pretty surprised I didn't drive Annie to quit. It was by far the most stressed-out period of my life.

The way I saw it, one second Amber and I were just having fun figuring out how to do the new-parent thing, and then the next moment the world came crashing down. It seemed like things couldn't get any worse. We were feeling sorry for ourselves, asking questions like, *Why us?*

Six weeks after the initial diagnosis, it was time for Beattie's surgery. Though we had been anxious for several weeks, after spending some time at the children's hospital in Winston-Salem, North Carolina, and meeting the parents of other children who were in much more critical condition than Beattie, Amber and I realized just how lucky we actually were. I had the realization that there's always someone who is suffering more than you. It was a valuable perspective that helped bring the color back to our outlook on the world.

From: Doc Hendley
To: WTW mailing list
Sent: Friday, November 14, 2008, 7:44 p.m.
Subject: News on Beattie

Well, it looks like the surgery was a success. I am actually quite jealous of my son already, because he is going to have the coolest scar on his head, much cooler than any of mine.

He is still in quite a bit of pain, especially when lying down, but he doesn't really pitch a fit at all. He's being a trouper. The surgeon removed a strip of his skull about 5 or 6 inches long from the front/top part of his head all the way back behind the crown of his head. She said in a few months new bone will begin to form in its place and that he will be perfectly normal now that he has a soft spot.

This whole thing has been tough on Amber and me, but after being in the children's hospital I am so thankful for what we have. There are so many other children and families out there that have problems I can't even imagine.

When Beattie was about halfway through his surgery, Amber and I saw a family get called into an office near the waiting room. Not a minute later we heard the mother sobbing uncontrollably. The doctors had been performing a fairly routine surgery on their little 2-year-old girl when something went wrong. The family, waiting just like Amber and me on news of their child, was told their little girl wasn't going to survive . . . Forty-five minutes later our surgeon came and told us Beattie did great and that his brain development and everything else is perfect.

I was relieved, but at the same time I ached for the family still mourning in the next room. I almost even felt guilty. Why did their child have to die? Why are any of those children in that hospital faced with such pain and suffering? There are so many things about this world that I do not understand.

I can't write in words how thankful I am that all of you have been praying for our son. I know that even if we were the ones that got the bad news, that we would have a great community of people waiting to support and love on us when we returned home. Thank you all so much.

Much Love,
Doc

P.S. If y'all would, keep praying for Beattie. He has about 2 weeks where he has to stay free from infection or any type of sickness. If he does get sick it could be very dangerous for him, because the surgery was so close to his brain.

Despite the successful surgery, Beattie was scheduled for a second operation nine months later. Our son was doing very well, but we weren't. Although we still had medical insurance through Amber's old job, the coverage wasn't nearly enough to take care of it all. The medical bills were mounting; Amber's student loan was due; she wasn't working; and I wasn't earning much with Wine to Water.

Soon we were more than sixty thousand dollars in debt.

Prior to that time, I was never one who believed in credit cards and debt. I had a near-perfect credit score and swore I'd never carry any debt. But now I had no choice.

Sure, Beattie's operations were expensive, but honestly, I would've been willing to pay millions of dollars and sink deeper into debt to take my son to the best doctors and surgeons in the country—whatever it took to make sure he was safe and well cared for.

That was when I had another realization. This one hit me square in the head like a ton of mud bricks. In many parts of the world, like the very places where Wine to Water works, there are lots of parents struggling (just like me) to provide for their children. But while we were going into debt over hospital bills, there are many parents who cannot even provide for their children the basic essentials for survival, like clean water. In reality, something as simple as a thirty-dollar water filter could provide clean water for their whole family for five years. But many can't afford that. And going into debt isn't even an option. What a helpless feeling that must be.

The reality weighed heavily on me.

But it was also empowering. Sure, I couldn't give those kids health care and top-notch education, but I did know exactly how to help them get clean water to drink.

So Annie and I pressed on with Wine to Water, hosting more fund-raisers, and I did as much public speaking as possible.

"Please book my calendar full," I said to Annie. "I don't

care who I'm speaking to—Kiwanis, churches, Rotary clubs; it doesn't matter. I just don't want to see any white spots on my calendar."

And so that was exactly what Annie did.

One evening I'd be speaking to a bunch of businessmen in suits and ties at some fancy dinner, then the very next morning I'd be doing a presentation for a bunch of kindergartners.

"What was it like in the desert?" one inquisitive youngster asked.

"It was dusty and hot," I said to the young boy. "And there were crazy sandstorms."

"Whoa! What's a sandstorm?" another kid asked.

"It's a huge wall of sand that would come and take over a village. There was lightning and thunder, and sometimes rain."

"Wow," the kids said, almost in unison.

"Did you see any lions?" a boy asked.

But I wasn't just doing speeches. In Cambodia, where about 74 percent of the country's deaths are directly related to the lack of clean water, we hooked up with a local organization to help drill wells in the country's poorest provinces, including an area called Svay Rieng. When we first began work in Cambodia we were operating in cooperation with local contractors to drill the wells, each of which cost twenty-five hundred dollars—the going rate that all other NGOs were paying for wells. But by working closely with the locals, in December 2008 we were able to purchase a drill rig made of local parts. Using that rig, we were able to reduce our cost per well to just five hundred dollars. We began drilling four wells per month, and soon were able to double our output to eight wells each month.

By involving the locals from each village in drilling their own wells, we were able to teach them the process and ensure that they would be able to fix their own wells using local parts should they break down in the future.

I had always hoped I could mold Wine to Water to be different from so many of the other aid organizations I saw while working in Darfur. Rather than simply shipping in teams of Westerners to fix the world's problems, I realized it was better to involve the locals themselves in solving their own problems. It was empowering for them, and much more cost-effective for my organization.

Still, even with huge cost savings like those we secured in Cambodia, Wine to Water was barely subsisting month-to-month. Obviously 2008 was a rough year for fund-raising, with the United States knee-deep in the Great Recession. Though my salary was officially forty thousand dollars, I drew only twenty-two thousand that year. Annie continued many weeks without drawing a salary too. And although I never verbalized this to her, I made a pledge to myself that if the Wine to Water account ever dipped below zero I'd take that as a sign that it wasn't meant to be and we should shut the organization's doors.

Many months we came really close—in the fall we got down as low as twelve dollars. But just when I thought it was all over, we'd get another sizable donation in the mail and we'd be back up and running, sending funds to our filter factory in Uganda, the well drillers in Cambodia, or wherever there was a need.

Then, the very next month, our balance would be hovering right above zero again. The stress was almost too much to handle. It's one thing to have a sick child—that's stressful, but at least you know it's not your fault. Financial stress, now, that's a totally different animal. I was constantly questioning my actions, and there's a lot of guilt associated with it. My family was already wildly in debt, and I wasn't about to do that to my organization too.

Miraculously we squeaked our way through 2008 and into 2009.

In early March, I got what I figured was a prank telephone call.

"Hello, is this Doc?"

"It is. Who's this?"

"This is Danielle Berger, from CNN," she said matter-of-factly. "I was hoping I could ask you some questions. Do you have a minute?"

Wine to Water had been receiving a small amount of publicity with articles in local newspapers when we hosted events, but it turned out Danielle wasn't interested in an interview. Apparently I had been nominated for the 2009 CNN Heroes award. Basically the network has an annual program that highlights everyday folks who are doing something to better the world. Viewers nominate and vote on the "heroes" and then they have a big awards ceremony to feature the top-ten heroes with the most votes. Prior to that day, I'd never heard of the program, and was equally surprised to learn that I was nominated by my old friend Tasha Craft, who had recently become Tasha Sullivan after marrying another one of my best friends, Ubie.

That phone call kicked off weeks of heavy vetting, as the CNN staff checked out Wine to Water's history, looked into our finances, checked my references, and more. Then, in late April, it was officially announced that I had been selected as one of the 2009 CNN Heroes, an honor I shared with twenty-seven other very deserving individuals.

From: Doc Hendley
To: WTW mailing list
Sent: Wednesday, April 29, 2009, 6:03 p.m.
Subject: CNN Heroes update

Hi y'all,

I wanted to send everyone an important update about how this stuff all happened . . .

About 6 or 7 weeks ago I got a call from some CNN lady saying that she wanted to ask me a few questions. I of course said yes, but asked why she wanted to talk to me. She then told me, "Well, you were nominated to be a

CNN Hero." I was obviously shocked, but then she told me: "Yeah, somebody from Raleigh named Tasha sent in this great story about you and we just want to get all the facts straight." Most of you know Tasha—but for those of you who don't, she was the first friend I made when I was living in Raleigh, and she is actually one of the main reasons I decided to leave Raleigh and do this work in the first place.

Tasha wrote CNN Heroes about 2 months ago on my and Wine to Water's behalf, and whatever she wrote must have been great, because there are thousands of people who are nominated and only a handful make it through. Besides owing her a huge "thank you" for the nomination, I owe her an even bigger "thank you" for believing in me 5 years ago and motivating me to travel and follow my dream. She had just returned from Africa herself when we first met, and in early 2004 she really helped me get this whole Wine to Water thing up and running. I can honestly say that I don't think any of this Wine to Water stuff would have ever happened if it weren't for her help and motivation in the beginning, and now we wouldn't have any of this great exposure if it weren't for her help again.

Thank you so much, Tasha, for everything!

Sincerely,

Doc

. . .

I was hopeful that the exposure with CNN could raise Wine to Water's profile and potentially lead to more donations. What I wasn't expecting was that I would be selected by an esteemed panel of judges, including folks like Colin Powell, Whoopi Goldberg, and Sir Elton John, as one of the top-ten most influential heroes on their list. That honor, and being recognized on national television as part of a huge gala event hosted by CNN's Anderson Cooper at the Kodak Theatre in Los Angeles, was one of the most inspiring and humbling times of my life.

CNN Heroes aired on Thanksgiving night and prompted a flood of new donations for Wine to Water. Prior to that, we had raised just under two hundred thousand dollars for the year, but in the next thirty-four days of 2009 we raised another two hundred thousand.

That exposure also led to more valuable publicity, including an interview on *Larry King Live*. It also set the stage to make 2010 a huge year for Wine to Water, enabling us to bring clean water to more people than ever.

NINETEEN

·····

It was mid-January 2010. I was headed back to northern Uganda to check in with our local team operating the Wine to Water training facilities in that region. I was a little uneasy about leaving home—Amber was eight months pregnant with our second son, and I wouldn't be around to tag-team with her on our now healthy and rowdier-than-ever Beattie. Still, part of me couldn't wait to get back out into the field. Logically, I knew that my office work was key to keeping Wine to Water going in the right direction, but being out there digging wells and interacting with the people we were helping made me feel alive, and was always a raw yet rewarding experience.

As I breezed through the Charlotte airport on my way out of town, the television monitors caught my eye. Apparently there had been an earthquake in Haiti. It wasn't an extremely massive one—7.0 magnitude. The damage reports were still a bit hazy, but I had a sick feeling in my stomach as I boarded the plane.

By the time I landed in Uganda, some twenty-four hours of travel later, my mind was focused solely on getting out to see our teams and projects in the field. It wasn't until three days later that I learned the full extent of the tragedy in Haiti.

I was in Gulu, a small town in the northern part of the country, eating breakfast at a tiny, ramshackle hotel and restaurant. A small color television hung in a dusty corner of the room broadcasting news from CNN about the quake. I was transfixed by the images of the capital city of Port-au-Prince. There were heaping piles of rubble where buildings once stood, and desperate looters rummaged for food while the police tried in vain to stop them. I watched as CNN reporter Anderson Cooper ran, carrying a young boy whose head was bleeding profusely. He'd been hit by a chunk of concrete hurled by the rioting looters.

The estimates of the damage, which continued ticking across the bottom of the screen, were staggering—well over a hundred thousand people dead and 1.5 million homeless.

Many more people are going to die if they don't get clean water in there, I thought to myself. *And there'll be twice as many dead if cholera sets in.*

Right then, I made the decision to leave on the next plane
out to try to get myself to Haiti as soon as possible. There was
much to do in Uganda, and I still had nine days left on my
itinerary there, but I knew Haiti was where I needed to be.
I called and changed my airline tickets immediately. Then
I spent the afternoon searching for someone who would be
willing to drive me the six hours, straight through the night,
to the airport in Kampala.

Meanwhile back in Boone, Annie, with help from our
newest team member, Chelsea, had begun organizing Wine
to Water events to directly benefit Haiti—which would
eventually raise nearly a hundred thousand dollars.

Because the airport in Port-au-Prince was closed, I had
to first fly into the Dominican Republic, which occupies the
eastern half of Hispaniola. Haiti occupies the western half.

About one week after the quake I was en route to Port-
au-Prince. Through some connections with the generous
owner of the largest radio station in the Dominican Republic, I was able to arrange for a helicopter airlift from Santo
Domingo into Port-au-Prince.

As we flew west over the border separating the two countries, the landscape abruptly changed. The Dominican Republic was verdantly green and lush, but because of rampant
deforestation, Haiti had dramatically less vegetation. It was
dry and brown, with clear-cut scars and lots of erosion. The
homes and structures, even in places unaffected by the earthquake, were markedly less well built and cared for than in the

Dominican Republic. The contrast of the two countries was striking—and sad.

The closer we got to the earthquake's epicenter, the village of Leogane, the worse the destruction became. Port-au-Prince was particularly hard-hit. Banking toward the airport, I could clearly see massive white-and-blue tent cities sprouting up throughout the city.

The scene on the tarmac was chaotic. International soldiers and humanitarian workers from all corners of the globe were desperately directing the flood of aid and supplies pouring into Haiti.

The thing I remember most was the stench. Haiti's humid air was heavy with the smell of decaying human flesh and burning bodies. It was sickeningly sweet, like a rotten pork roast that was burned in the oven. Combined with the stifling tropical air, the acrid odor literally took my breath away. My nostrils pleaded to be free from that putrid smell.

Nearby, towers of bottled water were staged near the runway awaiting distribution. Sure, some bottled water is necessary after a natural disaster, but in general I think it's one of the least sustainable methods of addressing a water crisis. Once that water was consumed, the bottles simply became mountains of litter covering the already trashed streets of the capital.

Without enough bottled water to go around, many earthquake survivors resorted to drinking water from the street gutters. More than one million folks were being exposed to deadly waterborne diseases such as cholera and typhoid.

Reusable water filters were what the Haitians needed most. That was exactly where I chose to direct Wine to Water's response. We partnered with FilterPure, a nonprofit organization out of the Dominican Republic that builds water filters. The filters were ceramic, simple things made much like clay flowerpots. Before the firing process, the clay is mixed with sawdust and a small amount of fine-grain silver. The sawdust burns in the kiln, leaving tiny porous holes for the water to trickle through. The silver mixed throughout kills any bacteria making it through the tiny pores. These pot filters, sitting inside a simple five-gallon plastic bucket, are capable of filtering water for a family of eight to ten people for up to five years.

Some folks from FilterPure picked me up at the airport in a truck loaded with filters. Together we started handing them out throughout the city, in refugee camps and at orphanages in the area.

Just like every other developing city I had traveled to, the traffic in Port-au-Prince was chaotic. What made it worse was the fact that probably half of the roads in the city were buried in rubble. Looking at the faces of our fellow drivers, it was clear to me that many of them were still in shock. Their stares were blank; their minds appeared muddled. Seemingly every day I witnessed pedestrians being struck and killed by the crazy traffic. It was mayhem.

In much the same way that Nyala was monochromatic, the city's buildings all the color of the surrounding desert floor, everything in Port-au-Prince had a gray cast to it. The toppled buildings and the streets were all the color of cheap cement. The bent rebar stuck askew from every pile of rubble, like fractured ribs protruding from a broken body. Everywhere there were power lines, electrical lines, and telephone lines, jumbled up into black bird's nests. On nearly every block, we would encounter flattened cars and trucks crushed under fallen buildings. A closer look and that telltale stench often revealed motionless bodies hunched over steering wheels and dashboards.

In the mornings and evenings when I wasn't delivering loads of water filters, I spent my time alone, walking throughout the streets of the capital. The morning walks were always the worst. During the night, stray dogs roamed the city, digging into the crumbled houses to feed on decaying bodies. The next morning, the streets were littered with half-eaten limbs, torsos, and heads that the dogs dragged into the streets. So every dawn, women who lived on those streets would collect the body parts and burn them in the gutters with piles of trash.

Much of my time in Haiti, I camped out on the front lawn of a deserted and heavily damaged international aid building. I wasn't about to sleep inside, so I pitched a tent, built a fire, and feasted on canned tuna and hot sauce while the mosquitoes feasted on me. Those nights reminded me of my time in Darfur.

From: Doc Hendley
To: WTW mailing list
Sent: Sunday, January 31, 2010, 6:46 p.m.
Subject: E-mail update from Haiti: lessons learned

Sorry y'all. This is long (please don't feel like you have to read it).

After another filter distribution in a run down camp here in Port au Prince, I decided to walk around the city for a while. I've been sick and tired of people talking about how dangerous this place is and how the Haitian people are out of control looting, fighting, selling children, etc. Since I have been here I have seen nothing but a devastated population that is trying the best they can to rebuild their broken lives. Their glares, mistaken as anger by all the expats, are more than likely just a look of despair, fear, and loss. So, when I'm not working with the filters I'm kind of wandering around aimlessly, just taking everything in.

Yesterday I saw a guy in the street who had just been killed. This city has become increasingly chaotic with all the military, organizations, and contractors who mainly have local drivers that are still in shock themselves over everything. So it's a recipe for disaster. The guy was just pulling out of his new tent home on his bike in the same camp where we distributed filters today when a truck hauling debris smashed into him and kept going like nothing happened. He was far from being able to be saved (I'll spare the details). But I was moved when his family ran out into the street as they heard the news. Here is a family that has been through hell and back these last few weeks and to make matters even worse their husband, father, brother, son, was just killed by a truck. I watched the whole family mourn out loud for a while and then continued to walk on my way as I asked myself over and over the simple question, "Why?"

Today I was wandering a part of the town that not many foreigners make it to. As I was passing by one of the countless destroyed buildings, I stopped for some reason to take a closer look. What caught my eye was a line of people, almost like worker ants, slowly clearing debris with 5 gallon buckets. I pulled out my little flip camera to film it when a man in broken English asked me to come inside. So I did. He explained to me that the building was their church and that no one had come to help them, so they, as a congregation, were clearing the rubble themselves one shovel full and one bucket full at a time. He also told me that over 30 people were in the church when it collapsed and none of them made it out.

While I was talking to the first guy, a young man of maybe 20 came up to me to ask a question. As he began to speak I noticed his whole body began to shake. It took him a while to get the words out, and when he finally was able to complete a sentence this is what he stuttered out:

"Wha-wha-wha-what are you doing? Wha-why a-a-are you here? Wha-why do you take the pictures?" I told him it was because I was intrigued by their hard work, and that maybe I could help by telling their story to people in America, and that maybe we could get them some help. He stared at me for a few seconds, and then it looked like he was about to cry when he said, "Ya-ya-you want to he-he-help?" He paused. "Then help," he said as he hold out a bucket for me to take.

"OK, you're right," I said, taking the bucket from him and making my way to the line of worker ants making their rounds hauling the very rubble that killed their loved ones. These people don't want trucks full of westerners coming to their "rescue" by kicking bags of food off a truck and leaving. They are people for God's sake and they need to be loved by us just like we would if a church, home, or school collapsed in our own hometowns. We wouldn't drive to the gates of that church or school and kick off a sack of food and then leave. We would walk right in the door and before we did anything else we would give them a big ol' freakin' hug . . . and then we'd strap our boots on, put on a pair of gloves and help them rebuild.

Thank you all for everything you do to support us and our efforts. And please toss some more prayers up for these people. They need 'em.

Doc

. . .

At the end of that first week on the ground, we dropped the last of our water filters at an orphanage in Leogane. The orphanage originally cared for a couple hundred children, but after the quake, the yard behind the building became a make-shift refugee camp for the entire surrounding community.

A two-doctor team (one MD from the States, one from Haiti) set up shop on the back porch of the orphanage. They were at capacity daily, sometimes treating over a hundred and fifty injured and sick locals a day. Unfortunately, they had no access to clean water to wash their hands or surgical instruments, so they were very grateful when we showed up with a load of water filters. That afternoon, the American doctor told me that 80 percent of the patients they were treating were sick from drinking contaminated water. It felt good to know that the filters we delivered would soon have a profound effect on those numbers.

For some, being immersed in the daily death and destruction of Haiti would've been the makings of a waking nightmare. For me, it was the completion of the circle. It was the realization of a dream I had six years earlier that night in my parents' home in Boone, North Carolina, back when I was nothing more than a bartender on the verge of stumbling onto his own destiny.

TWENTY

What?" I said into my cell phone. "Why won't they let them drive across? Clearly we are bringing supplies in to help their people!"

"The officials at the border are saying our guys don't have the right paperwork. Apparently there is some kind of new paperwork and we need that instead," said Lisa Ballantine, a U.S. expatriate who founded the FilterPure factory in the Dominican Republic.

"So did they get the papers?" I asked.

"Nope. The problem is, we don't even know what papers they're talking about," explained Lisa. "And none of the other

NGOs we've spoken with know anything about it either. I'm pretty sure they just want money."

"Screw that! I'm booking a flight down there now," I said, agitated by what I suspected was obvious government corruption. "I'll get the load across. No problem."

It was May 2010, more than four months after the earthquake and three months since my last trip to Haiti. Although our team had successfully imported about two thousand filters into the country from the factory in the Dominican Republic, Lisa and I decided that it made the most sense to establish another factory in Haiti. Building the filters there would be more economical, sustainable, and, most important, a good way to involve the local Haitians in solving their own country's water crisis. Once up and running, the factory would be capable of producing fifteen hundred filters per month, which could bring clean water to many needy families.

We were two months into assembling the factory in Jacmel, a seaside city in southeastern Haiti. All that was missing before we could begin production was that one last truckload of machinery that had been stopped at the border in Jimani.

Following the earthquake, the borders were wide open. It had been simple for us, and other NGOs, to get aid into Haiti. All of the government buildings had collapsed in the quake, so the officials were essentially out of work and no longer able to maintain their borders. Instead, UN peacekeeping forces took over. Fortunately, they were very responsive to letting aid organizations bring in supplies. However, as the Haitian government got back onto its feet and slowly regained control over its borders, many crooked border officials saw the regular international aid shipments flowing into their country as an opportunity to extort money for their own personal gain.

Still, I was sure I'd be able to get that shipment across without having to pay too large a bribe. I had learned a lot since first getting into water work back in Darfur in 2004. Besides learning to fix hand pumps, dig wells, and write grants—and the importance of involving locals in the work that we were doing—one of the most valuable lessons I came to know was that sometimes you have to work the system or fly under the radar if you really want to get something done. Whether it was meeting with Janjaweed commanders and essentially bribing them by fixing their hand pumps, or skirting the sluggish and often corrupt governmental bureaucracy by digging an unapproved wildcat well for a needy orphanage in northern Peru, I knew how to get things done.

Maybe it's a Robin Hood thing, or perhaps I've got some of my granddad's John Wayne in me, but I've never once felt guilty about bending the rules to bring someone clean water. The way I see it, water is the most basic human right. It is not a privilege. It sickens me to see how water sources can be wielded as a weapon or, perhaps worse, sabotaged by crooked politicians and greedy officials.

As soon as I arrived at the factory in the Dominican Republic, I had the guys immediately reload the truck with the supplies needed to complete the factory in Jacmel. I was going to get the job done. No crooked border officials were going to stand in my way.

Or so I thought.

When I arrived in Jimani, I encountered a long line of cargo trucks parked at the border. Some had been waiting there for more than a week. I also ran into the same bureaucratic roadblock that our guys had met with several days earlier. After I'd waited in line after line, the officials told me I didn't have the correct form or stamp, but they wouldn't, or couldn't, tell me how and where to get it.

I was stewing in the front seat of the truck. My frustration and anger had started to get the best of me when a young man tapped on my door. He was in his early twenties, wearing dark gray slacks and dusty brown leather shoes, with a faded blue dress shirt swallowing his narrow frame. It was obvious he was doing his best to look professional, but was too poor to pull it off.

"Hey, man, I help you cross," he said to me in an accent tinged with Creole.

I said nothing, just turned and looked the man in his eyes.

"You pay some money and I get you the stamp you need. Then you drive across."

As I mentioned before, I'm no stranger to bribery. At that point I was more than willing to ante up to get across.

"How much?" I asked.

"I don't know. You come," he said, gesturing for me to follow him back into the customs office.

This time we bypassed the long lines, and he escorted me into a simple air-conditioned office where a government official sat behind a large desk. The gray-haired man was in his early fifties and wore a neatly pressed military uniform. He was talking loudly into his cell phone, but paused to speak with my new escort. They spoke quickly and in French Creole. I understood nothing.

"He wants to know what you bringing in the country."

"Tell him he can see for himself," I said confidently. "It is equipment to make water filters so that his people can have clean drinking water."

The two men went back to speaking Creole. Then my escort spoke up: "He will let you cross, but you must first pay a tax."

"Yeah, yeah, I get it," I said. "How much? Hundred bucks? Two hundred?"

The uniformed man shook his head in disgust.

"Two hundred U.S. dollars? No, no." The younger Haitian chuckled. "More than two thousand U.S. dollars."

"Two thousand bucks?! Screw that! You tell your boss thanks, but no, thanks!"

In my younger days I might've caused a huge scene that would've landed me in prison, but something popped into my mind that stopped me.

I remembered an expat I met back in Port-au-Prince two months earlier when we were working alongside each other doing filter distribution. I recalled his telling me about a small fishing village near the southernmost Haitian border. From there he had taken a boat to Jacmel.

I quickly turned and walked out the door, then sprinted back to my truck. Suddenly I had a plan.

During the four-hour drive to that other border crossing, a call came in from Annie. She was telling me about a Wine to Water event that some supporters were holding for us down in Miami. Our organization had continued growing so quickly since *CNN Heroes* that Annie and I were no longer able to attend every Wine to Water event. We were gaining supporters in cities across the country, so we started walking people through the steps of how to hold their own Wine to Water fund-raisers. We put a checklist and downloadable brochures and posters on our Web site, and before we knew it, we were hearing from lots of people who were turning their Wednesday-evening book clubs or their favorite happy-hour nights into Wine to Water fund-raisers.

I was already energized by the growth in donations we'd seen. Witnessing people getting involved on such a grassroots level and taking ownership in Wine to Water made me realize that our organization had huge growth potential. To me, that was one of the biggest milestones in Wine to Water history.

By the time I reached the other border crossing, it was late afternoon. There were no trucks waiting, no officials presiding over long lines in the customs office. In fact, there were just two rickety portable office trailers and a high chain-link fence next to a small creek separating the Dominican Republic from Haiti. On the other side of the creek I could see much more activity, but still no lines.

A Haitian official in a well-worn military uniform strolled up to my truck, his eyes examining my load curiously. It was obvious these folks weren't used to seeing aid trucks coming through their border, the reason being that this border was on a road that dead ends at the sea. No one sent aid through there, because there was no way to get it on to Port-au-Prince and other needy areas. Local officials had yet to begin viewing aid workers like me as potential extortion targets.

The man simply asked me what I was hauling, and all I said was, "Aid for Haiti."

He looked my truck up and down once more and then motioned for a soldier to open the rickety gate.

I breathed a sigh of relief as I piloted my truck through the shallow washout and into Haiti. But that feeling didn't last long. There were tons of locals swarming the gate and my truck. The town seemed dustier than the Dominican side, and there was trash everywhere. Several young men jumped aboard the back of my truck to steal a quick ride, holding precariously to the wooden slats that kept my cargo from bumping out. I gingerly parted the crowd with my truck, then charged down the dirt road, headed for what I hoped would be that old fishing village that expat had told me about.

The road ended at the edge of the sea, where a collection

of small huts and shacks was built. There was one wide tree, and below it sat dozens of Haitians. Some were napping. Others played cards. Nearby, piles of cargo sat waiting to be loaded onto one of the four long wooden boats that bobbed just offshore.

Some locals started to perk up as my truck rumbled to a stop nearby. As I climbed out of the truck, all eyes were fixed on me. Seconds later I was swarmed by young men who had obviously deduced that I was looking to ship all that cargo in the back of my truck.

I spoke no Creole, but I was able to communicate enough to drive a hard bargain. After about an hour of yelling and feigning offense, I settled on a deal with a scruffy, bearded man in his mid-thirties who walked with a crutch. For three hundred dollars plus the cost of fuel, I paid for a captain and five men to load all of my supplies onto a thirty-five-foot-long wooden boat. In the end, the total cost of the voyage was significantly less money than the bribe the official in Jimani was demanding. I justified it all, knowing that my little aid-smuggling operation would be able to help support this poor fishing village in some way.

About the time the sun dipped into the sea, the rickety boat was completely loaded with all of my equipment. Much to my surprise, it easily swallowed my entire truckload with room to spare. I thought we'd get started on our seven-hour journey to Jacmel right away, but the captain just told me to wait. Then the porters proceeded to load three motorcycles and dozens of huge sacks of grain and beans on board. I was confused, because I thought I had rented the entire boat, but I didn't mind, as there was plenty of extra space. That is, until the load of thirty Haitians climbed aboard. I had to laugh as I was forced to jockey for just enough space to sit.

We departed around eleven p.m., and I noticed almost immediately that we were taking on water. From my perch, leaning against a fifty-pound bag of grain, I watched the young boatmen bailing bucket after bucket from our leaky hull. The old wooden craft groaned and creaked as we crested and descended the gentle swells.

I tried to sleep, but I couldn't. The stars wouldn't let me. There were millions of them piercing the moonless sky—the most I'd seen since looking up from my sleeping bag in the Darfur desert. The guttural *dut-dut-dut* of the boat's ancient outboard motor sounded like the Caribbean cousin of one of those old single-cylinder engines endlessly grinding sorghum in all those Darfuri villages. Even with an old snoring Haitian man falling into my lap, right then I knew there was nothing in this world I'd rather be doing. It was clear this was my calling.

The sun was slowly rising over the deep green hills of southwestern Haiti as the engine slowed and our boat glided quietly toward the beach. I made out the figure of Boyer standing there in the sand, the young Haitian man who was heading up our filter factory in Jacmel. He stood with his hands on his hips, looking out at the boat overflowing with passengers and equipment for our factory. He had a truck staged nearby, and I could tell from his body language that he'd been waiting there for hours.

His impatience made me smile.

There was so much work left to do, but I knew we would get it done.

Acknowledgments

Mark Anders: A very special thanks to you for helping me put my stories into words and those words onto paper. I truly appreciate your creativity, hard work, and dedication, and cherish the friendship we created through the process of writing *Wine to Water*.

Mom and Dad: Thank you for teaching me how to find the right path while at the same time allowing me space to be wild and free. I am forever grateful for your living expressions of faith and for showing me that how I walk is much more important than how I talk.

Tasha and Ubie: Thank-you for your unconditional love and friendship and for always believing in me, even when I doubted myself.

Dickson and Beattie: Thank you for being my heroes when I was a boy and for showing me how real men ought to live life.

Friends and family: A huge thank-you to everyone from my crazy cousins, to my crazy friends, to my crazy siblings, to my crazy crew at the Wine to Water office. You all remind me daily that life is entirely too short to be serious all the time and that being crazy is much more fun!

Samaritan's Purse: Thank you for giving me the opportunity to work in Darfur and for the chance to learn from your amazing staff. You have set the bar high in the nonprofit world, and have become a wonderful example of honesty and integrity for other organizations to follow.

Adam Korn: Thank you for seeking me out and encouraging me to write my story. I've had a blast getting to know you, and I look forward to drinking beers and talking MMA whenever I'm in New York.

Brian DeFiore: Thank you for being the best literary agent on planet Earth. Your wisdom and experience help even a country boy from North Carolina feel at home in the ever-growing and changing world of publishing.

Megan Newman: Thank you so much for being the absolute perfect editor for me. You knew exactly what I needed to hear and how I needed to hear it to stay focused and motivated throughout this whole process. I knew after our first meeting that we were destined to not only work well together but also to become great friends.

The Avery crew: Thank you all so much for working so hard to make this book what it is, especially Miriam Rich (Megan's more-than-capable assistant) and Lindsay Gordon (my faithful and awesome publicist).

Author's Note

This book is a work of memory buttressed by research. Any errors of fact likely reflect the dimming of recollection due to the passage of time.

Index